Praise for *Badly Beha*

Human behaviour can seem more (
This book investigates bad behaviour and how we can ᵣₛₑ ₐ__
achieve our dreams.

Dr Niamh Shaw, Irish engineer, scientist, writer and explorer; voted one of Ireland's leading science communicators and STEAM specialists (merging science, technology, engineering, arts and maths); she believes in dreaming big and is on a mission to get to Space

I've experienced badly behaved business leaders like the ones in this book. They default to 'telling' – viewing communication as one-way. As Greg Dyke, the former Director General of the BBC, said 'Leaders must first LISTEN to earn the right to be heard'. Successful leaders ask great questions and listen. They listen to WHAT is said, listen to what is NOT said and listen to HOW it is said. They don't need to know all the answers. Instead, they need to read Zena's book and learn the right questions.

Jeff Grout, leadership expert, listed in '*100 Best Business Speakers in Britain*'

Zena Everett brings incredible insights to this guide for anyone navigating today's complicated work interactions, much of it remotely, where misunderstandings are magnified, and generations are colliding. It is the best book on how to work successfully with other people that I've ever read.

Lauren Kelley, CEO, OPEXEngine by Bain & Company

There are so many life lessons and strategies to apply from Zena's book. Some chapters are quite painful to read (does that mean it's working?) and other chapters feel like a warm hug. Come with an open mind and get ready to learn what makes people behave badly in the workplace. So many unsavoury characters are described, and Zena helps us navigate dealing with them - or indeed stop being them ourselves! And come out on top.

Helen Banks, Entrepreneur and Founder of Imperfect Pointes

Whilst we are still working with human colleagues, Zena is the workplace agony aunt we need.

Mariel Juhlin, Entrepreneur, Innovation Manager and AI expert

In Zena's brilliant writing style, she has distilled a huge amount of complex information into a practical and enlightening guide. I recognised my own 'idiotic' leadership behaviours within these pages and had a few 'aha' moments regarding some challenges I've faced with badly behaved bosses.

Her advice about selecting a coach to address your own challenges is spot on, do your due diligence. Cost isn't a guarantee of quality! A good question to ask is if they have a coach themselves, known in professional terms as a 'supervisor'. If not, alarm bells should ring!

An entertaining, insightful, and well researched book that 'tells it as it is', highly recommend.

Rachael Hanley-Browne, EMCC Global Council Chair

A must read for anyone who wants to improve their relationships with others - and themselves! I loved the fact that it is evidence based without the psychobabble, and was amusing and fun to read, but also hugely insightful.

Dr Marie Stopforth, Chartered Coaching and Sport Psychologist

I live with an invisible difference which affects my processing abilities. I'm working on speaking up more and learning not to see 'everything' as a problem. This book will continue to nourish my tired mind, tired especially of people making assumptions about my capabilities as a neurodivergent person. I loved the format; it is clear, engaging, to the point and with helpful subheadings to navigate. Thank you, Zena for really listening.

Martha Jones, MA (Oxon).

People behave badly because they don't listen. I am a care experienced girl. I was told repeatedly that I should apply to work for the gas board. They didn't listen, I wanted to act. 'You'll live on beans on toast for the rest of your life' I was told. "I quite like beans on toast actually," I replied. My first acting job was Mary the Punk in EastEnders, the West End followed, as did more telly. Then I started to write for BBC science. A girl with no maths or English. I decided I wanted to work in tech. 'How can you work in tech, you're just a soap actress', I was told more than once. Read this book and learn how to stop giving or receiving advice we don't need. Everyone needs to be seen and heard.

Linda Davidson, BAFTA and Woman of the Future nominated, Woman in Tech; co-founder of Outside Thinkers, advocating and creating opportunity for care experienced people.

I loved 'Badly Behaved People' - it's an invaluable handbook for all of us at work. Zena manages to convey complex psychological and emotional theories about our behaviour with humour and humility. The book is a wonderful exploration of creating meaningful connections at work, and how each of us can take healthy perspectives on our behaviour and that of the people we interact with daily. As a fellow coach, I particularly resonated with the chapter on the coaching profession. Here Zena champions the importance of robust contracting, evidence-based coaching, and the importance of coaches maintaining a deep and curious knowledge of the human mind.

Lucy Whitehall, MA MAPPCP, Coaching Psychologist.

This book is a testament to soft power—the audacity to inspire and guide rather than tell! Zena masterfully explains how to course correct malfunctioning humans. This is an unputdownable read!

Alina Addison, author of *The Audacity Spectrum*

Zena is like Emily Blunt, offset behind Meryl Streep in The Devil Wears Prada - giving you discreet and timely intel on your next human interaction, whether at work or in life. You don't need sack loads of emotional intelligence; you just need Zena at your back. This book nudges you into making the necessary course corrections whenever "it's not me, it's you", which, let's face it, is most of the time. The book treats you to reality checks and nuggets that encapsulate instincts you already have, so you *feel* like a better manager as well as *being* a better manager. Zena made me feel proud of my scrappy career and now has me looking forward to tweaking the culture wherever I land next.

Lisa Rajan, author of 32 children's and YA books; former politician and journalist; six-time marathon runner

Everett's wisdom transcends all workplaces and industries, showing that ultimately, our careers are about people. In understanding our colleagues better, particularly those who don't share our own values, we can learn to flourish at work - no matter what we do.'

Ella Dove, journalist, author and TEDx speaker

Atomic reading! The reader is wrenched into self-awareness on every page. This is a must have at hand resource for anyone engaging with others, on how to nurture and sustain healthy habits and relationships in our lives.

Ingrid Tennessee, Chief Executive Officer and Non-Executive Director, Charity sector

For many years I have tried to give the affected a voice with the Kinsale Peace Project, bringing many of those affected by wars, hunger, poverty, torture or discrimination to my local community and schools to tell their story. I loved the stories in Badly Behaved People. Zena explains how much of the conflict the rest of us experience is in our own heads. We all need to spend more time listening to each other and ourselves.

Padraig Fitzgerald, Founder of the Kinsale Peace Project, Ireland

Another wonderful book by Zena Everett which explores the psychological underpinnings of 'bad behaviour' and shares a host of practical strategies to support more effective relationships for both those exhibiting and those dealing with 'bad behaviour'. Recognising that these behaviours are psychological learned coping mechanisms often worsening under stress, she highlights the need for Coaches who are working in this area to be accredited; well trained in psychological processes and evidence based coaching and to be able to thoroughly contract around coaching goals, expectations and the boundary between coaching and counselling. I endorse her view and think this is a great resource for those in the workplace and Coaches alike.

Wendy Oliver, AC accredited Master Executive Coach and Supervisor

Zena offers effective approaches to dealing with complex behavioural issues. As a psychotherapist turned coach, I found a goldmine of practical tools and questions.

Colleen Mizuki, Coach to the US Military, Department of Defense, Department of State, non-profit and high-tech organisations

All problems are people problems. Until workplaces provide everyone with their own psychiatrist, I suggest everyone reads this book to learn how to boost their self-awareness and understand their own – and other people's – bad behaviour.

David Goldstone, CEO and Founder, VOCASO and Goldstone Associates; investor, NED

As a senior HR leader in investment management who helps leaders become better leaders whilst tackling my own leadership conundrums, I found this book to be a game-changer! It was practical and easy to apply in everyday situations inside the workplace. I especially liked the style of the book, it has case studies and searching questions - the fact that I could dip in and out, focusing on what was needed was great.

Assumptions can be made about bad managers and leaders and that it is mostly "their fault" and they needed to improve - this thinking is challenged, and I had to ask myself what others were or were not doing to contribute to their unhappy situation, soon realising that the accountability didn't lie fully with leadership. I found myself thinking a lot about self-awareness, ownership and emotional intelligence. Great book, perfect for a busy leader or manager as well as HR teams.

Dimple Mistry, FCIPD, Human Resources Leader, Board Member, Ally

Badly Behaved People

Pearson

At Pearson, we have a simple mission: to help people make more of their lives through learning.

We combine innovative learning technology with trusted content and educational expertise to provide engaging and effective learning experiences that serve people wherever and whenever they are learning.

From classroom to boardroom, our curriculum materials, digital learning tools and testing programmes help to educate millions of people worldwide – more than any other private enterprise.

Every day our work helps learning flourish, and wherever learning flourishes, so do people.

To learn more, please visit us at **www.pearson.com**

Badly Behaved People

How to deal with idiots at work

Zena Everett

Pearson

Harlow, England • London • New York • Boston • San Francisco • Toronto • Sydney
Dubai • Singapore • Hong Kong • Tokyo • Seoul • Taipei • New Delhi
Cape Town • São Paulo • Mexico City • Madrid • Amsterdam • Munich • Paris • Milan

PEARSON EDUCATION LIMITED
KAO Two
KAO Park
Harlow CM17 9NA
United Kingdom
Tel: +44 (0)1279 623623
Web: www.pearson.com

First published 2025 (print and electronic)

© Pearson Education Limited 2025 (print and electronic)

The right of Zena Everett to be identified as author of this work has been asserted by her in accordance with the Copyright, Designs and Patents Act 1988.

ISBN: 978-1-292-73946-5 (print)
         978-1-292-47144-0 (ePub)

British Library Cataloguing-in-Publication Data
A catalogue record for the print edition is available from the British Library

Library of Congress Cataloging-in-Publication Data
A catalog record for the print edition is available from the Library of Congress

10 9 8 7 6 5 4 3 2 1
29 28 27 26 25

Cover designed by redeyeoffdesign.com

Print edition typeset in 10/14 Charter ITC Pro by Straive
Printed by Ashford Colour Ltd, Gosport

NOTE THAT ANY PAGE CROSS REFERENCES REFER TO THE PRINT EDITION

"Where there's a secret," she says, "there's shame – and shame is something we can do without."

Claire Keegan, *Foster*

Contents

—

I send bottomless love and gratitude to my family, friends and everyone I've worked with over the years. Thank you for forgiving all my bad behaviour.

While we work hard to present unbiased, fully accessible content, we want to hear from you about any concerns or needs with this Pearson product so that we can investigate and address them:

- Please contact us with concerns about any potential bias at https://www.pearson.com/report-bias.html

- For accessibility-related issues, such as using assistive technology with Pearson products, alternative text requests, or accessibility documentation, email the Pearson Disability Support team at disability.support@pearson.com

About the author

International leadership coach and in-demand conference speaker Zena Everett is the author of *Mind Flip: Take the Fear out of Your Career* and the award-winning *The Crazy Busy Cure*. Zena has a reputation for practical takeaways and evidence-based content delivered in a very entertaining way.

Photo by Claire Ballard

Originally a recruitment entrepreneur, she sold her business and studied an MSc in Career Management and Coaching and other post-graduate qualifications in psychological coaching and leadership. She has coached on the Executive MBA Programme at Oxford University's Saïd Business School and is a member of the associate faculty at Henley Business School, UK. Her focus is on replacing bad behaviour and crazy busyness with productive, thriving and profitable team relationships. Zena divides her time between her homes in London and West Cork and wherever her work takes her.

This is a short bio because Zena believes that real success comes from flipping our focus away from ourselves, and onto the problems that we, uniquely, can solve for others. It's not about us and our egos: it's what we can do for others that matters. Find out what she can do for you at www.zenaeverett.com and please get in touch with her if any of her stories resonate with you: zena@zenaeverett.com

Introduction

'One of my workmates goes ballistic at the slightest hiccup. How can I put the pin back in the grenade?'

'Why can't people take criticism anymore? I feel I'm working with a bunch of fragile snowflakes.'

'My manager gushes to me about my work but stabs me in the back to others. How can I work with her, let alone trust her?'

These dilemmas are the stuff of my work as an executive and leadership coach. I listen to people's ambitions and the frustrations that block their way and then ask questions that build self-awareness about how we respond to challenges. It may sound like a simple job, but it's not. It may sound as if I'm a paid bystander, and I'm not that either. I'm on the pitch with my client, without being a player, an umpire or a team shrink.

I'm there to listen without judging and smooth the way to better understanding. Coaches like me help our clients to untangle crossed wires and reconnect. Their underlying problem is universal: we place bad behaviour at someone else's door, feeling we are the most sensible and thoughtful person in the room. Yet sometimes we are the ones with the crossed wires.

Imagine this book as a laboratory petri dish, showcasing the curious conduct of people who remind you of your colleagues and, more crucially, highlighting puzzling elements about your own behaviour.

You'll read dilemmas from my coaching practice to illustrate why people behave badly and see how to cope when they do. Some problems will resonate with your own experiences. You'll discover and curb your own idiotic tendencies too; we all have them since we're all human.

I have strategies to help you through rough patches, often where you may struggle to communicate with colleagues. Persistent blocks of this kind can be exhausting, chipping away at your self-esteem, as if you were a poor frog being boiled slowly.

I will also share the searching questions I use with my clients, helping you to adopt a more coach-like approach in your own relationships so you can help others to grow.

If you are a leader already, this book will help you become a better one. But it doesn't matter what your job is, you can become the wise person people gravitate to when they need precious space to think: the best listener in your workplace.

I hope you enjoy the book and I'd love to hear your stories: please get in touch at zena@zenaeverett.com.

Chapter 1

Most problems are people problems

When you ask someone how their work is going, they say little about what they *do*. They talk about how work makes them *feel*: the energy of the workplace, the team dynamics, how they fit in, whether they trust their boss, which colleagues muck in, and those who don't. They talk about who they get on with and who drives them crazy.

What matters most about our jobs are the people.

But people aren't just that clichéd 'greatest asset' of an organisation, they are also its greatest headache. We work in an interconnected world. We work with, for and alongside other people. I work for myself, but I work with clients, agents, collaborators, associates, editors – and I have a bank manager to please.

Diagnosing the reasons for people's puzzling behaviour is usually the major topic of my coaching sessions. Sometimes the problem is a lazy colleague, a moody manager who snaps for no obvious reason or a colleague who has stolen ideas. Even when my client is a manager who has hand-picked their team, people surprise them. Superstars don't always meet expectations. Experienced hands sometimes reject constructive feedback.

I haven't named this book *Bad People* because most of the people featured here aren't bad, although I have at least one extremely unpleasant character. Most problems involve 'normal' people behaving badly under pressure. Tension at work is not always a problem; it's a useful part of our day, keeping us on our toes, boosting our performance and helping us to shine.

What's crucial is how we react to pressure. Trying to protect ourselves from it simply encourages behaviour that upsets others and ignites the blue touch paper.

It's easy to spot when people are behaving like idiots. And we can fall into the idiot trap ourselves.

Can we change our behaviour?

Absolutely. Once we are aware of what we're doing, we can change.

Can you change other people's behaviour?

Absolutely not, although the idea sounds lovely. We only control our own behaviour. But if we change the way we behave, others might just change the way they behave around us.

How do work relationships really work?

We need close, trusted work relationships as much as we do at home. At the heart of every organisational success story is a high-performing team bound by a shared purpose. They may not want to socialise and there might be friction between team colleagues. But they function well together. Good leaders build strong teams by creating this shared – ideally visceral – bond with the group's objectives, along with a higher purpose as their touchstone.

In May 1961, US President John F. Kennedy committed to the ambitious goal of landing a man on the moon and returning him safely to earth before the end of the decade. 'We choose to go to the moon in this decade and do the other things, not because they are easy, but because they are hard,' he declared. Yet the US had yet to send a man into space and bring him home.

The Soviet Union had already put the first man-made satellite into earth's orbit in 1957, triggering the Space Race that became part of the Cold War. The month before Kennedy's famous speech, the Soviets sent cosmonaut Yuri Gagarin into the earth's orbit and brought him back home.

The US was in the Soviet Union's rear-view mirror.

The following year, during a visit to the NASA space centre, the President noticed a janitor carrying a broom and interrupted his tour, walking over to the man. 'Hi, I'm Jack Kennedy,' he said. 'What are you doing?' The janitor replied: 'I'm helping to put a man on the moon, Mr President.'

Which of these superpower nations won the race to put a man on the moon? The US, of course, helped by a leader with ambition and the gift of oratory, backed by a driven team, all of them bound by the same purpose.

Having a shared sense of group identity is vital to our chances of survival. The prehistoric part of our brain doesn't want us outside the cave, vulnerable to prey. We perform better when we feel safe, when we belong, all of us pulling in the same direction. A united tribe has a better chance of survival than one caught up in constant disagreement.

Research in psychological safety, carried out by Amy Edmondson, Professor of Leadership at Harvard Business School, shows that the most successful groups have enough mutual trust to share vulnerability and take risks in pursuing their group's goals. Having a best friend at work makes us better at our jobs and more likely to stick with them. We don't want mindless harmony, just healthy, competitive friction and a shared commitment to making a difference.

A good business recognises that a strong, connected culture is a vital starting point for success, not a by-product of it. People are the difference between success and failure, not tools and processes. A Harvard study of more than 200 companies found that a positive company culture can increase net income by 765 per cent during a ten-year period.

Human resource departments do their best to create motivational, connected, safe spaces for 'employee stakeholders', as staff are now called. Good vibes . . . smiley faces . . . kombucha . . . foosball tables . . . gym memberships . . . awaydays . . . sleep pods . . . Organisations try whatever it takes to keep their greatest assets in top form.

The jury is still out on how to create these vital group bonds when we're no longer working in the same place. Great brains and focus groups – often called 'innovation clusters' these days – are puzzling out the Zoom equivalent of a 'water cooler moment' that creates these essential connections.

Does the theory work in real life?

Yes. Man has walked on the moon many times since JFK's landmark speech. Several nations have worked together to build the International Space Station as a science laboratory, and we use earth's orbit for satellites we rely on daily. Tremendous achievements, but we need to do better.

Are you working for Darth Vader?

Professor Robert Hogan, an international authority on leadership, invented the Hogan Personality Assessment tool, which measures the dark and light sides of our personality. He reports that 80 per cent of working Americans are stressed about their jobs, with 75 per cent saying their immediate boss is the major cause.

Are your managers a daily downer?

Stanford University psychologist Teresa Amabile studies how everyday life at work influences people and their performance. Her research covers creativity, productivity, innovation and the mix of emotions, thoughts and motivations that govern how we work. When managers came up in her research, staff saw them as a demotivating factor.

Are you logged on, but zoned out?

Gallup's *State of the Global Workplace 2023 Report* found that nearly 90 per cent of UK employees are emotionally detached from their jobs because they feel they don't belong. Globally, nearly six in ten workers felt the same. They may be in the office, logged onto their computers, sending out emails, but don't know why their work matters. Nor do they have healthy bonds with their colleagues, boss or the organisation that pays their salaries. Gallup estimates the cost of this disengagement to the global economy is US $8.8 trillion, 9 per cent of global GDP.

People are openly quitting, or worse, quietly quitting – employed but doing the minimum. They have a resigned attitude without leaving the job. They aren't doing the deep thinking and problem-solving that's vital for business success. Why?

Organisations rely on big experiences when creating culture: hyperbolic speeches and culture transformations. What matters to the rest of us is our 'lived experience' – we'll ignore the annoying tautology – our relationships and the behaviour of others. The annual conference doesn't light our fire; the small stuff does.

We live our lives day to day, not in the Rah! Rah! awaydays because real life is, well, real. It's messy. It's the everyday interactions that upset us, while the grand mission statement leaves us cold. In the same way that marital relationships break down gradually and end in divorce, it's the small niggles in the workplace that bring on the resignation.

Likewise, it's the everyday interactions with our colleagues – especially our managers and leaders – that create the connections we crave. The everyday interactions that show the good or bad behaviour of others are the ones that make, or break, us.

This may seem small stuff, but we can't help sweating it. We rarely see our incompatibility with colleagues through one big bust-up, but through regular, tiny signals. What people say. What they do. The stuff that filters through to how we feel.

Being social animals does not make us the same animal family. We may not be in sync with our tribe. We may not share the same values or work ethic, and we are unlikely to want to hang out socially with all of our colleagues. Some people will like us, others won't.

Artificial intelligence may be our strategic challenge, but people are our real-time problem. You might long to work with robots who'll wash up their own mugs, but you're stuck with fallible human beings for now. Humans are complex, illogical, moody, stressed, emotional, imperfect and sometimes childish. We have irrational feelings. Our wires get crossed. We bring emotional baggage to work.

Take this classic cock-up, an email sent by a university's payroll administrator one December in response to guest lecturers chasing overdue invoices in time for Christmas.

Hi Team

Thank you for your email & apology for delay in Payments [sic].

We are sorry to let you know that Bacs Payment run dates are not yet scheduled and remittance will be sent out as soon as Bacs Payment runs is completed in our system.

Best wishes

Who is to blame for this? The payment system? Of course not. You blame the insensitive idiot who didn't solve the problem and then fired off this thoughtless email. Or maybe you blame the insensitive idiot's useless boss who hasn't trained them. The culprit is a person, not the software.

The Post Office *Horizon* scandal is the most widespread miscarriage of justice in British history and represents the biggest single series of wrongful convictions in British legal history.

Faulty accounting software created false shortfalls in the accounts of thousands of subpostmasters – the entrepreneurs who owned and ran more than 9,000 Post Office branches. Between 1999 and 2015, more than 700 subpostmasters were wrongly convicted of theft, fraud and false accounting. The victims and their families suffered an horrendous personal toll, resulting in illness, divorce, loss of livelihoods and homes, bankruptcies and at least four suicides.

Post Office senior executives claimed the software was robust and could not be accessed remotely without the subpostmasters' knowledge. Executives used racist language to classify subpostmasters suspected of theft.

Eventually, a whistleblower admitted the Fujitsu's Horizon software was flawed and could be accessed without the subpostmasters realising.

Convictions have since been quashed; a statutory public enquiry is still unravelling how the injustice remained hidden for so long.

Faulty software? Yes. Bad behaviour by people in two separate organisations? Absolutely.

Our behaviour is getting worse

We have a lower trigger point, post-pandemic, for a mix of reasons.

Long days facing a screen suck the life out of us; we just aren't built for it. And it doesn't stop at the end of our working day. Business becomes personal when it disrupts your personal space, like those incessant messages that ping while you try to have a normal life.

Misunderstandings happen more easily with 24/7 connection, when communication isn't always face-to-face. A beer or two followed by a hastily sent message and we soon discover a line-up of people we've annoyed or who've wound us up. Isolation offers more time to over-think a minor irritation into a big eruption.

We. Are. Tired. It's hardly surprising since we face a relentless schedule of energy-sapping meetings. 'Change fatigue' is now a problem. Count the transformation projects going on around you; compare that number with the equivalent five years ago. I've seen entire teams ground down with what psychologist Martin Seligman calls 'learned helplessness', exhausted and losing the impetus to challenge unacceptable behaviour or put forward their point of view.

People shrug their shoulders. 'What's the point of trying? That's the way it is here.' We've lost any energy and eagerness for healthy friction and fresh thinking.

Who's the real problem here?

Could it possibly be us? Is our frustration justified? Is it everyone else who behaves badly? Or do we behave like idiots sometimes?

Ninety per cent of conflicts can be resolved without the involvement of others, says Professor Steve Peters, a consultant psychiatrist and bestselling author of *The Chimp Paradox*, a bestselling book that offers a mind management model to help us become happy, confident, healthier and more successful. How can we refuse?

Maybe we are the problem for everyone else but can't see it. Are we the micromanaging control freaks annoying our team? Perhaps we're the bottleneck who sits on everything, delaying everyone else from getting on with projects?

How often do we question our blind spots? Do we talk over others? Have you noticed how those who complain most about other people's behaviour are the most badly behaved?

Is the conflict in your own head?

When there's no one else involved, the bad behaviour can only be self-inflicted. Our own mind is the enemy, caught up in daily friction with the sneering inner voices that make us behave illogically. We sabotage our chances of success by the way we think.

There are three common traps: we talk down what we can achieve; we assume the worst will happen; or we worry excessively about what people think of us. The result is we avoid taking risks to stay safe and avoid failure and humiliation. None of this helps our team or us, since we're not aiming high enough or performing as well as we can. We're cruising, maybe not quite in neutral, but close enough. Our attitude can infect the entire team.

How does this self-sabotage show up? Maybe you're rejected at a job interview and assume it's because you aren't good enough for the job. You've been exposed as punching way above your weight. A big ouch! So, you apply for jobs more junior than your existing one, and you don't get these because you're coming across as mad for aiming low. Would it ever occur to you that you didn't get the first job because the interviewer felt you would move on quickly because you were too good and weren't being stretched enough?

What should we make of this scenario? A colleague had a barbecue last weekend, and while other team members were invited, you were left out. Do you assume they just didn't want you to come, that everyone hates you? Well, maybe that's true . . . But they might think you are so far out of their social league they didn't want to embarrass themselves by inviting you and hearing you make a flimsy excuse. Or maybe you've been quiet, consumed by doing a great job on a big project, and your colleague assumed you weren't interested in socialising.

Jumping to the conclusion that feels the most hurtful drives you to behave unfriendly at work. Now your colleagues really dislike you, and your nagging inner voice says: 'I told you so!'

How do I know when it's not them, and not me either?

Sometimes, no one is a real problem. The bad behaviour is a mash-up of mutual misunderstanding. The problem lies in the way we interact with each other, the crossed wires of what happens between us.

If this reminds you of your intimate relationships, you've grasped my point. No matter how 'professional' we try to be, we see unhelpful thinking, biases, dramas and illogical behaviour just as much at work as we do at home. We only have one flawed brain we take everywhere. Even if we keep a professional lid on our behaviour, our subconscious is still tick, tick, ticking, often making irrational guesstimates, and reacting to others from lopsided conclusions.

We are creatures of emotion, not logic. We subconsciously set up situations that reinforce our ideas – healthy or not – of where we stand in the world. Others will see us repeating the same patterns in our private life, not realising that we can see their patterns too. Why does everyone I love always do a disappearing act? Well, continuing to date known philanderers and being surprised when they leave is likely to be the answer. Same behaviour, same outcome.

At work, we may feel we are a put-upon 'goodie', and someone else – or even the entire organisation – is the 'baddie'. We feel resentful and increasingly behave in a hostile way, asking for conflict to show up. The story plays out as it would in a movie, although we don't change as heroes do in a movie to earn a happy ending. We cling to our flawed thinking and nagging inner critic. We get stuck in our own story.

Early life influences

Most of the bad behaviour I see in my coaching work comes from one or more people in a conflict cranking out unresolved childhood issues that govern how they see the world. Like it or not, we are often talking with a vulnerable child stuck in a grown-up's body. That adult sales director in the sharp suit sitting in front of you is often wearing a mental nappy. Our backstories matter. Not our career histories, but the beliefs we develop in our early years that influence our relationships now.

Many of us have unrealistic expectations from other people; we want them to fill the emotional gaps left from our childhood. Some of us keep working for nasty bosses, projecting unresolved issues from our earlier lives onto a destructive work alliance. I've met perfectionists and workaholics desperate to satisfy unpleasable people from their past – most likely their parents – by subconsciously recreating that dynamic with authority figures at work. Desperate for validation, they work harder or better than everyone else, hoping in vain for the attention they've always craved.

Walter Isaacson wrote a biography about the complicated late Steve Jobs, co-founder of the trillion-dollar triumph that became Apple. Jobs was known both for inspiring those who worked with him and for tearing them down.

Isaacson wrote of the time when his parents dropped Jobs off at college. Jobs didn't say goodbye, or even thank them. Later, he admitted how ashamed he felt about his behaviour. He'd simply wanted to be like an orphan with no roots, no connections and no background.

His wish had identifiable origins. Jobs had been adopted by Paul Jobs and Clara Hagopian, unaware of his biological roots. When Clara died, he sought out and met his biological mother and sister Mona. He often ate in a restaurant without realising it was run by his biological father, a man who later told *The New York Times*: 'All of the successful technology people used to come there. Even Steve Jobs . . . he was a sweet guy and a big tipper.'

When the connection between the men emerged, both kept their distance, one for fear of being exploited, the other fearful of being thought a fortune hunter. Is it any surprise that Jobs see-sawed between being a visionary and a petulant, angry child?

The legacy of our earlier lives can be devastating. Charles Spencer, brother of the late Diana, Princess of Wales, wrote a memoir about the physical abuse he suffered as a child at his exclusive British boarding school. He believes many people at the peak of politics are likely to have been brutalised at similar schools, leaving them with mental scars which continue to feed into their decision-making. Earl Spencer suggests these dog-eat-dog systems inflict repetitive cruelty that leaves pupils cruel in their judgement of what's right and wrong, something that shows up in the work they do today.

Based on our childhood experiences, we form irrational ideas which can crowd out other people's point of view. We look for evidence that confirms how we see the world. Life is cruel . . . we must please everyone . . . only the tough survive . . . people cannot be trusted . . . I'm not good enough . . .

We can't see reality, only how we *want* to see events to meet our needs and perpetuate our often-irrational narratives. We project skewed motives onto people's behaviour and cannot see their point of view. We act badly, suspiciously or just plain weirdly, and we get what our slanted view of the world teaches us to expect.

We make unreasonable demands of others and ourselves. We expect people to think and behave as we do, to share our values and to be motivated by the same things. Problems spring up when we make assumptions about people based on our own view of the world.

Comedian Ruby Wax studied mindfulness-based cognitive therapy to understand her own depressive episodes, turning the results into a series of serious and funny books about her discoveries. She writes in *Sane New World: Taming the Mind* that we become so trapped in *our* interpretation of the world that we are prepared to go to war with others who are trapped in *their own* world view: a war of warped realities. Who's right, who's wrong and does it matter? To quote the late Queen Elizabeth II, 'recollections may vary'.

I don't believe people intend to misbehave. Stephen King, bestselling author of scary books, ought to know about bad behaviour. And he knows about bad writing too; he declares simplistic writing comes from a stubborn refusal to face the fact that 'murderers sometimes help old ladies cross the street'.

No one ever sees themselves as the baddie. Most of the time, they're right. They just behave in ways that damage other people – or themselves. Sociopaths and psychopaths – and a few of Stephen King's characters – are exceptions. Coaching can't stop them from violating the rights of others; you won't meet any of them in my client stories. Sociopath and psychopath are genuine labels from the psychiatrist's bible, the *Diagnostic and Statistical Manual of Mental Disorders*, or DSM book.

I'm focusing here on 'idiots' we meet in the workplace.

I have a confession to make. Idiot isn't a label I'd ever use. It makes for a compelling book sub-title, and it's used daily in common parlance, often in anger. But I'd never dream of calling someone an idiot and neither should you. People just behave idiotically. It's vital to separate who we are and how we behave. And we can change our idiotic behaviour once we are aware we're doing it.

Increasing our self-awareness is the first step. Once people understand how their mind works and nudges their behaviour, they are on the way to fixing their problems.

This book is about the complex interplay between people. It will make you better equipped to read people more fluently. You might blush as you recognise versions of yourself. Don't worry; none of us is perfect.

Resources

Amabile, T. and Kramer, S. (2011) *The Progress Principle: Using Small Wins to Ignite Joy, Engagement and Creativity at Work,* Harvard Business Review Press.

American Psychiatric Association (2022 edition) *Diagnostic and Statistical Manual of Mental Disorders* (DSM-5).

Coyle, D. (2019) *The Culture Code,* Random House Business.

Daisley, B. (2020) *The Joy of Work: 30 Ways to Fix Your Work Culture and Fall in Love with Your Job Again,* Random House Business.

Gallup (online) State of the global workspace. See: https://www.
gallup.com/workplace/349484/state-of-the-global-workplace.
aspx (accessed 3 July 2024).

Hogan (online) Hogan assessments. See: www.hoganassessments.
com (accessed 3 July 2024).

Isaacson, W. (2015) *Steve Jobs: The Exclusive Biography*, Abacus.

Kotter, J. and Heskett, J. (1992, reprint 2011) *Corporate Culture and Performance,* Free Press.

Patel, A. and Plowman, S. (2022) The increasing importance
of a best friend at work. See: https://www.gallup.com/
workplace/397058/increasing-importance-best-friend-work.aspx
(accessed 3 July 2024).

Peters, S. (Paperback, 2021) *A Path through the Jungle
(A Psychological Health and Wellbeing Programme to Develop
Robustness and Resilience)*, Mindfield Media.

Radicati (online) Email statistics report. See: https://www.radicati.
com/wp/wp-content/uploads/2023/04/Email-Statistics-Report-
2023-2027-Executive-Summary.pdf (accessed 3 July 2024).

Seligman, M. (2018) *Learned Optimism: How to change your Mind
and your Life,* Nicholas Brealey Publishing.

Spencer, C. (2024), *A Very Private School,* William Collins.

Wax, R. (2013) *Sane New World: Taming the Mind*, Hodder &
Stoughton.

Chapter 2

———

How to use takeaways from the stories

In the stories that follow, I am going to introduce you to the stars of the book like Hotshot Harry, Toxic Tina and Underperforming Ellie. I've either coached them or their manager. Reading about how we untangled their problems will help you to gain a better understanding of yourself and other people – and develop your coaching intuition. That means learning to listen, to ask questions and to be more self-aware and emotionally intelligent.

The dilemmas show us useful lessons.

- All our problems are people ones, but you know that already. Sometimes it's them, sometimes it's us and sometimes we over-think ourselves into believing a non-existent problem is real. Issues fester until we understand each other. We need the courage to ask someone for their perspective, without assuming we can read their minds.

- We can only change our own behaviour and how we respond to others. When we do that, people often meet us in the middle. Or they might not. Madness lies in thinking we can fix other people or get them to think the way we do. They aren't us and we aren't them. People often ignore what we say, but copy what we do; life is a spectator sport.

- The leader of a group's dynamics may not be the most senior person in the room. Just as one rotten apple can ruin the whole barrel, one good, powerful personality can galvanise an entire team by asking questions, listening and restoring trust. Don't underestimate the influence you, your moods and your actions have on everyone else, regardless of your place in the pecking order.

- The people problem you see first is rarely the key one, so jumping to solve it without grasping the full picture only tackles the symptom – at best. It may even make things worse. Maybe Tina isn't that toxic – although she probably is – and maybe Harry isn't obnoxious after all. Horrible though it feels, maybe the real problem is how you interpret reality. It's easy for us to project your own baggage onto your work experience. Your client doesn't hate you just because they haven't replied to your email. They just haven't replied to your email yet. Discover the facts before leaping to judgement.

- Most of us try to show up to work as our best self, behaving in the professional way expected by our job title. We might try to separate our work and private selves or choose to be genuine and show personal vulnerability. Whatever your choice, it's often our five-year-old inner child that reacts to stress, not our grown-up version. Recognising that the other person in our conflict may show up as a similarly emotional child is an enormous step towards emotional maturity.

- Solving other people's problems demands a diametrically opposite approach to solving business problems. In your day job, you're an expert, paid to have a set of expertly honed skills and a relevant opinion. When diagnosing people problems, you need to do the opposite. You're now an amateur, not an expert. We can't know what's going on in the mind of someone else. Suspend judgement, empathise and listen with an open mind to show you care. Knowing the right question to ask is more valuable to the other person than thinking you know the answer to their problem. You might need to unlearn some habits and it can be tough.

The dilemmas coming your way aren't scripts you can follow to get through a coaching exam; this isn't a coaching manual and I'm not claiming to be the best coach in the world. That's not self-effacing imposter syndrome, which comes up a lot in the stories. If you are a qualified executive coach or a veteran armchair psychologist, and you think you'd have handled these cases better, then you are undoubtedly right. But I'd argue there's no perfect outcome, just the one the client wanted.

If you think I got it wrong, that my take on their interpretation is wrong, you're proving my point. Take it from Nietzsche himself: there are no facts, only interpretations. We're burrowing into misunderstandings, irrational beliefs and crossed wires: conflicting narratives between people. I'll explain about our flawed thinking as we go: we are all prey to it and it's the root of bad behaviour.

You'll notice the dilemmas and coaching questions could apply to multiple situations. I've used a mix of questions to keep the process interesting but also to give you choice. I have skipped goal-setting models because we are shedding light on bad behaviour here, rather than coaching for performance improvement.

The dilemmas are real ones, drawn from my coaching experience. You'll meet a large and diverse cast of characters, anonymised to protect identities and preserve their privacy. But I'm sure you'll recognise similar people from your day job. I've done my best to avoid patronising cookie-cutter stereotypes; forgive me if you think you've found some.

There are people problems I haven't included here for space reasons or because they haven't cropped up in my coaching practice. In no way does that reflect any lack of significance.

The issues are relatively straightforward and focus either on a single issue, or on one issue for each of the people involved. I've condensed timeframes. You are smart enough to grasp that life is more complex and nuanced than it may appear. No silver bullet exists to shift deep-rooted problems in the blink of an eye.

Most problems need both practical and psychological mediations. Who doesn't have unresolved childhood issues that gnaw away at us, prompting our irrational behaviour? It's just that some of us manage these better than others.

The people you'll read about are what psychologists call 'the working well', those in good mental shape, even if the way they think isn't always as logical or emotionally intelligent as it might be.

I'm not qualified to navigate complex psychological disturbances. That's different from coaching. Venture into another person's acute psychological issues or trauma without suitable training, and you may harm both of you. I cover this as it pops up in the relevant dilemmas.

Please seek specialist support if you need help with any of the issues covered in the book.

How to view the stories

Each dilemma starts with my brief from the client. That is the coachee – the person being coached – or whoever is sponsoring coaching in their organisation. Then I list the major theme, the topics that come up in our coaching.

Spot when you see discrepancies between their interpretation of the problem and the reality of it. Does the client really know what's going on or are they making assumptions? As you'll see repeatedly, our perception of a situation is mostly a projection of our own reality. We can't outrun our back story: how our early experiences frame the beliefs we hold about ourselves and other people. These cloud our perception of what's actually happening. The good news is that we can change those deeply held beliefs about how we view the world and our place in it. We just have to do the work.

Try to notice:

- if you make swift judgements
- if any situations strike a particular chord with you
- if anyone especially irritated you and why
- if the outcome you expect differs from what happens
- if you would have done the same in their place.

Questions and listening – not answers

At the end of most dilemmas, I offer useful questions for similar scenarios. You can try using them on others, or just on yourself.

If you are flexing your own coaching muscles, don't head down the rabbit hole of looking for the 'perfect' question. There's no such thing. Listen hard and don't think about your next question. It will come. Even better, work in the silence while you think of what to say next. Quiet space in which to think is a gift.

Listening, giving someone your full attention and then asking questions instead of suggesting answers is harder than it sounds. Biting your cheeks and not interrupting someone is an enviable skill. I keep my opinions to myself unless asked for them; my client knows the best answer to their challenges, not me. Staying in the role of being an empathetic sounding board isn't easy. It's tempting to stop listening and start paying attention to your own thoughts – 'it's obvious what's going on here, so let's speed this up a bit by telling them'.

How many people do you know who really listen to you? Next time you are in a meeting or social situation, time how long it is before someone interrupts your conversation with: 'Oh yeah. That happened to me as well. What you should do is . . . '

Knowing when to shut up, and when to speak up

From an early age, some of us are taught to be seen and not heard. Learning to speak up is career-enhancing. Being assertive and able to express our views well moves us up the career ladder.

But remaining silent, actively listening and asking thoughtful questions can empower others to find their own solutions. If only these qualities were as appreciated in the workplace as being loud and 'confident'.

If coaches aren't paid for opinions, what do we really do? Our role is to challenge people's assumptions and conclusions, to help them consider where they may be wrong, or missing the other side of a story – or at least a good chunk of it. We help them challenge someone's interpretation of their dilemma and find any blind spots. Between us, we find their unhelpful patterns of thinking, review the options where a decision needs to be made, help them choose the best one and then let them crack on with what they need to do.

Most of all, my job is to make people feel valued, cared for and safe during the time we spend together. Giving voice to what's on their mind enables people to come up with clearer strategies than if they simply thought about their problems.

It's the same as fully mastering a complex issue by explaining it to someone else. The difference between doing it with a coach and doing it with your best friend/boss/colleague/partner/pet is that a coach is objective. The others have skin in the game. Their partiality will always emerge, much as they might deny it.

Coaches are there to clear the way for someone to think in a neutral and un-manipulative way. We have no vested interest in where someone ends up, only that they achieve their goals. We are not leading anyone to a conclusion we feel is the right one for them.

Never assume. Ask and be curious

Finally, let's nail a myth. You might think it's all about stepping into the other person's shoes. WRONG.

You can't imagine the perspective of another person; all you're doing is imagining yourself as them. Except you aren't them. They have unique experiences, values, tastes, aspirations, mindsets, heritages and perspectives. People treat them differently than they would treat you. They started in a different place from you. If you try to put yourself in their shoes, you have only half the story, along with the likelihood of forming wrong and stereotypical assumptions. Here are assumptions we want to avoid.

• You think you have typical Gen-Z snowflakes in your team, complaining about not being heard and needing constant handholding. Do they have a point? Are you really paying attention to what they say? When you were at their stage in your career, you may have had to work everything out for yourself with little or no training, but it is a different world now, one with more complexity. Have you given them adequate instructions on what you want them to do and the reasons behind it? Who knows, they might discover a more efficient way of doing the job – if you spend time with them.

- Your team hasn't told you they are unhappy, so you are stunned by negative comments on the annual engagement survey. Have you asked them how they are and what they want? Several times? People don't speak up if you don't ask them first.

- Someone has declined your invitation to a watersport-driven awayday, followed by a booze-up. You interpret this as a lack of commitment or team spirit. You even feel hurt, thinking they don't like you. Might the truth be that they can't swim, or team sports intimidate them, or they don't feel comfortable in swimwear in front of colleagues? Perhaps they don't drink and don't want a hard time for staying sober. They aren't you.

- One of your team leaves their camera off during a meeting, so you assume they are still in their pyjamas. They might be, but they might simply need to keep their personal life personal. Maybe they aren't feeling well or have a cat that wants to hog the spotlight and they don't want the tail swishing to hijack the meeting. Or maybe their Wi-Fi is ropey.

- Someone doesn't make direct eye contact and you think they're shifty or brought up badly. They're good at their job, but you can't promote someone lacking in social confidence. After all, you taught your well-mannered children to make eye contact at an early age. Perhaps they are neurodiverse and find eye contact difficult or distracting?

- You assume others will make the same life choices as you did. A client of mine said her CEO assumed she'd make the same career choices as his wife had. Just because she had caring responsibilities it didn't mean she wouldn't take on a promotion or relocation, but it was taken for granted that she couldn't cope with them so she was never given the opportunity. Ask someone what they want. Don't assume you know the answer.

All you are doing when you put yourself in someone's shoes is making snap judgements from a subjective and often misguided perspective. It's a mental reflex called a 'fundamental attribution error'. In his book *Belonging: The Science of Creating Connection and Bridging Divides*, Geoffrey L. Cohen describes this as an impulsive cognitive bias that sees the behaviour of a person as coming from an 'underlying essence' – who you *think* the person is – instead of understanding that the situation they are in is what creates their behaviour. You don't know the full picture, what's going on beneath the veneer.

Instead of imagining the reason for their behaviour, ask them. Social psychologist Nicholas Epley calls this 'perspective-getting' instead of 'perspective-taking'. Ask people for their perspective and discover the context guiding their behaviour; don't just imagine it.

Behaviour change can also be a sign of mental health issues. Don't assume someone is fine because they say they are. Ask, and ask again – in person, not through a text or as part of a survey.

Regulating your own emotions like this and understanding the emotions of the people around you are crucial workplace skills. We'll explore how to raise your own empathy and self-awareness in the next chapter.

Resources

Cohen, G.L. (2022) *Belonging: The Science of Creating Connection and Bridging Divides,* W. W. Norton & Co, p. 107.

Epley, N. (2014) *Mindwise: How We Understand What Others Think, Feel and Want,* Penguin.

Eyal, T., Steffel, M. and Epley, N. (2018) Perspective mistaking: accurately understanding the mind of another requires getting perspective, not taking perspective, *Journal of Personality and Social Psychology* 114(4): 547–71.

Chapter 3

Everyday
emotional intelligence

Bad behaviours in the workplace come from low levels of emotional intelligence. Let's translate the jargon: EI is the vital ability to tune into and manage your emotions, understand the emotions of people around you and react rationally. It sounds easy, but putting it into practice is a different matter.

If you have high levels of emotional intelligence, the grown-up version of you will show up when an argument is brewing instead of the five-year-old child who wants to stamp their feet, scream and throw things around. You'll be able to face any crisis with lower stress levels, you'll react with less emotion and more objectivity. And you won't say 'How on earth did this happen?' when you find yourself down a rabbit hole you would have preferred to avoid.

Join me on a tour of emotional intelligence essentials; you'll gain quicker insights into where people are going off the rails.

My go-to bible of workplace behaviour is *Work Psychology*, by John Arnold, Professor of Organisational Behaviour in the School of Business and Economics at Loughborough University. It's an invaluable book.

Arnold defines emotional intelligence as 'a set of characteristics and styles that is thought to enable a person to utilise intellect, emotion and awareness of other people in his or her day-to-day behaviour'. I like the emphasis on day-to-day events since these are the ones that matter most in our relationships.

It's pointless to have someone's undivided attention in a career appraisal every six months, only to find that same person talking over you for the rest of the year. Connection builds day by day and strengthens gradually. Familiarity shouldn't breed contempt; it should breed trust. And trust builds our psychological safety, the key to high performance.

When American psychologist Daniel Goleman first published his best-selling book *Emotional Intelligence* in 1995, he turbo-charged an explosion of interest around the topic. Managers stopped rolling their eyes at the mere mention of someone's 'emotions' and began turning up at workshops on how to tune into them.

Academics argued about which was the best indicator of a colleague's job performance: emotional intelligence or 'ordinary' IQ?

Was someone's emotional quotient measurable? Or teachable? And was it even new – we already had personality profiling and trait theories, so was EI simply 'old wine in new bottles?'

Goleman defined EI as 'abilities such as being able to motivate oneself and persist in the face of frustrations; to control impulse and delay gratification; to regulate one's moods and keep distress from swamping the ability to think; to empathise and to hope'. He described it as a learned ability – so yes, it was teachable – that led to outstanding performance when mastered. It was a stirring discovery. We'd already landed men on the moon by then; perhaps we could control something vital and closer to home: our emotional reactions.

In 1990, Drs Jack Mayer and Peter Salovey declared that traditional measures of intelligence weren't enough; EI mattered. Our existing idea of intelligence had to include this extra element of interpersonal awareness and our ability to access and understand emotions.

Following those early days, academics spilled a lot of ink on how to define and measure emotional intelligence. From a practical standpoint, we know EI is the secret sauce of career success. People hit a ceiling when they lack these essential people skills. They can come off the rails because of it, destroying years of hard graft. We became certain that soft skills are as important as the so-called hard ones.

People who haven't learned to be emotionally intelligent struggle to relate to others sensitively. They lack self-awareness and empathy and fall prey to their own flawed thinking, behaving in unhelpful or downright damaging ways. They might think that being outstanding at the nuts and bolts of their job is enough. But it's not. They still need the gift of being able to relate to others. We rely on accurate data to do business, but we must be able to read the room too.

Being emotionally intelligent can strain the brain, just like your daily Wordle can drive you nuts. While writing this chapter, the phone rang: it was a friend, wanting to catch up. I had to switch between my frontal lobe, which does the analytical thinking, to the middle part of my brain, the amygdala, which is the social part. We're not aware of the switch, but it still happens.

Dr Matthew Lieberman is a UCLA Professor and Director of the Social Cognitive Neuroscience Lab. His neuroimaging studies show that when one brain region moves up a gear or two, the other one slows down. It's hard to engage in social, emotionally intelligent thinking at the same time as doing the technical part of your job, and vice versa. He calls this the 'neural seesaw'.

Most of us prefer to use one of these two networks over the other. This can become our default way of thinking, our instinctive way of behaving; you can't blame your bad behaviour on this. Neuroscience has proved that our brains are trainable like any other muscle. I can't blame my grey matter for a grisly response to a distraction. I'm in control of my behaviour and the impact it has on others.

The business impact of managing our emotions can't be under-estimated. James Zenger, CEO of Zenger Folkman – a firm specialising in driving leadership effectiveness and business results – surveyed 60,000 employees on what made an outstanding leader. Leaders strong in analytical and problem-solving skills were rated 'great' by *14 per cent* of employees. Leaders strong in social skills, such as communication and empathy, were rated 'great' by *12 per cent* of the employees.

However, the rare leaders who mastered the dance of the neural see-saw, strong in both results focus and social skills, were ranked 'great' by *72 per cent* of their employees. Emotional intelligence matters.

And what about the 28 per cent who wanted even more from their leaders? See them as a valuable lesson for everyone who falls into the trap of being a people pleaser: you can't make everyone happy, and there is the proof.

Everyone needs strong emotional intelligence. We all need to influence others, to get along with people and persuade them to see our point of view. When people can't do this, their careers stall, or worse, they head over a cliff. Whatever our professional goals, who doesn't care about establishing and maintaining meaningful relationships? We are social animals, and our relationships matter.

The problems offered here feature people who can't behave in a professional, emotionally intelligent way that fits their job description, even though that's a minimum requirement.

Perhaps they don't take responsibility for their mistakes, listen to feedback, respect boundaries or release control. They may have admirable intentions, but let their emotions take over when under stress. They confuse what's happening now with past painful experiences and all judgement veers off-piste. They act in the way they learned long ago to cope, none of which is healthy behaviour in the present. All of this shows up as bad, petty, unhelpful, nasty or plain idiotic behaviour. That's why the highly paid executive having a tantrum in front of you is reacting like a toddler. These people are entertaining to read about, but frustrating, even hideous, to work with.

How do we learn how to master EI?

Goleman broke down emotional intelligence into four intrapersonal skills.

1 **Self-awareness**: understanding ourselves, our motivations and characteristics.
2 **Self-regulation**: controlling our behaviour and acting with care.
3 **Social awareness**: understanding and empathising with other people.
4 **Relationship management**: managing and navigating our relationships.

Sigmund Freud, the renowned founder of psychoanalysis, said: 'The self we know is hardly worth knowing'. That's why most coaching programmes kick off with a feedback exercise to expose the gap between how we see ourselves and how others perceive us. It's a vital piece of the jigsaw to help us understand ourselves better.

On the following pages, you'll discover models for self-regulation – how my clients slow things down and learn to separate the stimulus or perceived stressor, and their behavioural response to it: *That person said something dumb. I can choose to let it go, not bite their head off for it.* We can't control how we think, but we can control how we behave.

We learn how to ask people for their perspective, not assume we know it. They feel validated and we have more empathy with them. Clients learn to navigate their work relationships, tolerating idiotic behaviour or calling it out when necessary. The aim is to work towards shared goals in a productive, respectful way. Sounds easy, doesn't it?

Rate yourself now on each of the four factors of emotional intelligence and see if your score improves by the end of the book.

Resources

Arnold, J., Coyne, I. and Randall, R. (2020) *Work Psychology: Understanding Human Behaviour in the Workplace*, Pearson.

Goleman, D. (2020, new edition) *Emotional Intelligence: Why It can Matter more than IQ,* Bloomsbury Publishing.

Lieberman, M.D. (2015) *Social: Why our Brains are Wired to Connect*, Oxford University Press.

Matthews, G., Zeidner, M. and Roberts, R.D. (2003) *Emotional Intelligence – Science and Myth,* MIT Press.

Mayer, J.D. and Salovey, P. (1997) 'What is emotional intelligence?' in Salovey, P. and Sluyter, D.J. (eds) *Emotional Development and Emotional Intelligence: Educational implications,* Basic Books.

Zenger, J.H. and Folkman, J. (2019) *The Extraordinary Leader: Turning Good Managers into Great Leaders* (2nd edition), McGraw-Hill Education.

Case studies: Managers behaving badly

Chapter 4

Why can't he control
his temper?

'Dear Zena

We need to talk about Kevin's uncontrollable temper. He literally loses his shit when the slightest thing goes wrong. He's a decent guy, but his outbursts are off-the-charts unacceptable. We say we are a 'people business', but how can we be, with this going on? If Kev can't control himself, he'll have to go. Is there a way to tackle his low trigger point?'

Themes

- Emotional regulation
- Emotional intelligence
- Anger management
- Amygdala hijack
- Stress management

Workplace conflict costs UK organisations £28.5 billion a year – about £1,000 for every worker. The cost includes loss of productivity, informal resolutions or early intervention, mediation, time off work, as well as formal procedures, dismissal and resignation. And we mustn't forget the prospect of litigation.

Then comes the risk of reputational damage. You can't cover up this type of behaviour these days. It's catnip for social media and sites like Glassdoor, where you can do more than search for an attractive job: you can read the anonymous verdict of people who've worked there.

An explosive Kevin is not just an unpleasant manager to work for, he's a risk too far.

Kevin was a regional director in a national estate agency/realtor chain. His HR director, who sent me that exasperated email, felt it was only a matter of time before someone would register a major grievance about his behaviour. Without realising it, Kevin was threatening the entire organisation with expensive, stressful and time-consuming disciplinary processes and tribunals.

When things went wrong, Kevin erupted to express his frustration. None of it was a personal attack or abuse. He didn't swear at anyone or belittle them, nor did he bear grudges the way a narcissist does.

Kevin simply exploded at the entire world when things went wrong. His outbursts weren't a full-on, eloquent King Lear rage against the storm; they bore more resemblance to a raucous 'why am I surrounded by effing half-wits!' declaration that no one dared try to answer.

Kevin wasn't intimidating nor was he a bully, but where this behaviour might once have been a rite of passage that might have been seen as encouraging colleagues to 'man up', today it's inexcusable.

I witnessed one of his outbursts. A team member videoed it, possibly expecting Kevin to morph into a green, Hulk-like brute. I can only imagine the sleepless nights the HR director had when he found out that the outburst had been recorded.

I expected Kevin to be a grumpy old dinosaur – I know, I know, my bias is showing. But he wasn't: he was delightful. He was a grown-up person in every respect other than anger. He just had a massive blind spot about this facet of his behaviour and the impact it had on others.

He'd grown up with 'bad-ass' bosses. In August 2009, the irreverent gossip site Gawker, which has since been shut down, published an article titled *The 10 Most Terrible Tyrants of Tech*, a list of screamers, chair-throwers, death-threat makers and the ones who 'get biblical on your ass'. Great for reality TV. Inspirational for screenwriters looking for Shakespearean villains. Just not fun in real life.

People just won't tolerate this behaviour now. When companies say people are the bedrock of their success, they mean it. Every training course – along with books like this one – bangs home the message that a manager's job is to create a safe environment where motivated people can flourish with trust and respect.

When three words say more than 'I love you'

Kevin knew all of this but hadn't joined up the dots about his tantrums sabotaging the great work he did. I needed proof. I couldn't show him the video, because it had been safely deleted, and the person who recorded it didn't want to be identified.

So I carried out a simple, anonymous feedback exercise with Kevin's team. I explained he was on a leadership development programme, and we wanted feedback to help him improve.

I asked the standard three questions that get to the core of an issue, questions that generate far more effective answers than long surveys that bury the message.

1 What more did they need from him?

2 What was he doing well?

3 What could he stop doing altogether?

I also asked everyone to describe Kevin in three words.

There was no ambiguity in the answers. They were more detailed than I expected, which showed that people weren't frightened of speaking up and genuinely wanted to help Kevin.

The patterns were that he was kind, always happy to have conversations with team members and was supportive. However, people were losing respect for him because he couldn't control his outbursts.

The three words included 'angry' (several times), 'explosive', 'weapons-grade fury' and 'dramatic'.

I once carried out a similar exercise where 'dark triad of narcissism, Machiavellian and psychopathy' came up several times in mixed combinations. That was a tough conversation.

I collated the feedback and showed it to Kevin. My work was done. As soon as Kevin saw the feedback, he was shocked into changing his behaviour. He was mortified at how his outbursts upset others. Until seeing the feedback, he had no clue.

Not only did he realise that losing his temper was bad enough, he saw how much worse his outbursts were for junior members of staff who felt unable to speak to him about it. His children were now young adults, and he said he'd hate for them to experience something similar at their workplace.

At his next regional meeting, Kevin thanked everyone who had offered feedback. He apologised for being 'an arsehole' and declared his intention to change. He said if anyone caught him swearing in future, he would make a £100 donation to the company's charity.

He earned respect from his team for the way he owned up to his bad behaviour. This was a straightforward exercise because Kevin changed his behaviour as soon as he was aware of it.

That's not always the case.

Emotional regulation: tune in and chill out

Emotional intelligence is the ability to tune into our own feelings and the feelings of others. Learning these soft skills is as important as learning the so-called hard ones relating to the specifics of our job. Mastering our emotions is a big part of being emotionally intelligent.

People with low emotional intelligence dip into a state called an 'amygdala hijack'. The amygdala – an almond-shaped structure in our limbic system – is the seat of intense emotions like aggression and fear. When these emotions flood, blood pressure escalates and wham! Someone blows their top just as Kevin did.

After an angry episode, people often excuse themselves, saying they can't help it, or that they are highly passionate people or are stressed, trying to make everything perfect. They might blame others for provoking them, or for failing to show appreciation or support.

I've coached several entrepreneurs with anger management issues. They all felt being a creative genius was an acceptable excuse for shocking behaviour; they couldn't help being upset with people who fell short of their high standards. Of course, they could – and should.

I'm partial to some fruity language myself, but shouting or swearing *at* others is never okay. We might not be able to control how we feel, but we absolutely can control what we do. There's no excuse.

Dominance comes from controlling emotions. If a gorilla can stay calm under pressure, so can we. The silverback gorilla, the type with the highest status, has been found to have lower levels of cortisol – the stress hormone – than others in the group. Granted they have considerable weight to throw around, but they have also mastered their response to stress and keep calm. Neuroscientist Tara Swart married this kind of scientific rigour with universal truths in her book *The Source*.

Resources

Goleman, D. (2020) *Emotional Intelligence: Why It Matters More Than IQ*, Bloomsbury Publishing.

Leeds, A., Schook, M.W., Dennis, P.M., Stoinski, T.S., Willis, M.A. and Lukas, K. (2023) Urinary oxytocin and cortisol concentrations vary by group type in male western lowland gorillas (Gorilla gorilla gorilla) in North American zoos. *Primates* 64(1): 65–77. See: https://pubmed.ncbi.nlm.nih. gov/36472720/#:~:text=Oxytocin%20concentrations%20 were%20greater%20in,males%20in%20other%20group%20 types (accessed 4 July 2023).

Swart, T. (2020) *The Source: Open Your Mind, Change Your Life*, Vermilion.

Watt, K. (2023) The canary in the mine: what the release of Acas data tells us about our workplaces. See https://www.acas.org.uk/ the-canary-in-the-mine-what-the-release-of-acas-data-tells-us-about-our-workplaces (accessed 4 July 2024).

Chapter 5

My team can't take criticism

'Dear Zena

HR has told me I'm brutal when I give feedback to my team, but I'm just telling it like it is. What's wrong with these lightweights? We've got targets to reach and need to crack on. Can't they take criticism?'

Themes

- Feedback skills
- Over-used strengths
- Listening skills
- Autocratic leader

If you find yourself typing 'am I too sensitive?' into search engines, the answer is most likely a firm NO. You are simply at the wrong end of someone's lack of emotional intelligence: in this case, you're facing a manager like Rohit.

Rohit's father was a plain speaker with high standards and everyone in his large family knew where they stood with him: tough love, he called it.

As a schoolboy, Rohit was a keen saxophonist. His teacher made no secret of what he thought about Rohit's performances, good or otherwise, especially when Rohit failed his audition at a prestigious music school.

Rohit didn't fulfil his musical ambitions elsewhere; it was all or nothing for him and he refused to stick around in a lesser college and work slowly toward a higher rung where he'd already failed. He couldn't bear rejection or disappointing others, so he found another way of getting approval and building his self-esteem.

He found it in the tech industry, where he channelled his energies into smashing sales targets. That lead to rewards, recognition and

promotion. He'd found his safe place, one where he could excel –
until he was given a team to manage.

Rohit took on his role with gusto, but his tactics of getting great
sales results by barging through doors weren't any help when it
came to the subtleties of managing people.

He prided himself on being transparent about everyone's
performance, often starting feedback sessions with the comment:
'I'm not going to lie'. To Rohit, this was simply tough love. He spent
most of his one-to-one chats telling people where they were going
wrong – something they already knew – but never asked questions
aimed at finding out why someone was underperforming or offering
help that would raise their game.

Rohit didn't find giving feedback difficult; he enjoyed telling
people exactly how it was. His attitude was simple: *'Hey, they
shouldn't be in sales if they can't handle criticism; a bit of tough talking
never did me any harm'*. What he found difficult was any show of
vulnerability or emotion from the person being berated. He quickly
shut down these conversations. He had a simple answer to this
dilemma: avoid hiring 'over-sensitive' people.

Rohit didn't want his career to end in shame, like UK politician
Dominic Raab, who'd been elected as a Conservative MP four times
for the southern constituency of Esher and Walton. Once inside the
Houses of Parliament, Raab served on three committees, and held
ten senior government posts, including Deputy Prime Minister at
the same time as serving as Lord Chancellor and Secretary of State
for Justice.

At one time, with Prime Minister Boris Johnson in intensive care
with Covid, Raab was a heartbeat away from the most important
government role in the UK, at a time when a global pandemic was
running amok. He'd previously been the UK's Foreign Secretary
and Brexit Secretary. No one could accuse the usually softly spoken
Raab of being a slacker; he was known as a hard worker, often from
7.30am to about 10pm, Monday to Thursday, with constituency work
on Friday and regular weekend work.

Even so, Raab stepped down as Deputy PM and Lord Chancellor
and Secretary of State for Justice in April 2023, after an independent

inquiry investigated complaints involving 24 people about his 'consistently abrasive behaviour'.

Civil servants gave evidence claiming they were so petrified of disagreeing with him that some felt physically sick before meetings. He was accused of 'hard staring' and interrupting staff with a raised hand when he'd heard enough. Raab described his leadership style as 'inquisitorial, direct, impatient, and fastidious'. He'd promised to resign were the enquiry to uphold any complaints, and he kept to that promise. In a testy resignation letter, Raab said he hadn't intended to cause distress, but merely wanted to raise inadequate standards.

The UK media were divided on whether Raab was a villain or a victim of a stitch-up by lazy snowflakes, perhaps because only two of eight complaints were upheld. One letter in a national newspaper said: 'Sadly, we are being driven by a generation that sees a raised voice as abuse'.

Like Raab, Rohit's plain speaking was – at best – being taken as searing bluntness. Most of his team avoided him, apart from their fortnightly one-to-one or at a team social. They rarely asked for his help, even though he might have been a valuable source of information and advice.

Of course, Rohit's no-filter style wasn't helping his team to improve, nor did any of them appreciate his regular rebukes. We had hard data and feedback he couldn't deny. His team said he was a fun guy, brilliant on a night out, but they wanted career development. They knew about their performance gaps; their straightforward sales roles made that easy to map. What they wanted was coaching from their manager to help bridge these gaps. Even Rohit's top performers were frustrated; Rohit lavished them with lots of back-slapping praise, but they wanted support to clinch their next career move.

Rohit needed to wake up to the impact his style had on others. He'd never had good leadership himself, so he was unaware of how transformative it can be. His personal coping strategy was his ability to push through tough times, but the thick skin he grew to make headway had become his problem. He wasn't oblivious to people's feelings; but they made him feel embarrassed. His team wasn't the problem; his lack of sensitivity to them was.

Wherever you sit in this debate, ruthless 'telling it like it is' simply isn't a passable leadership style now. Old-school macho leaders like Raab and Rohit earn short-term obedience, but that's all.

Putting people through excessive stress raises their cortisol levels. This shifts their brains either to make poor decisions or to freeze. Or walk. People leave autocratic leaders and those who've lost control. Rohit needed to change his communication style and his definition of leadership, part of which ought to include succession grooming. He risked being up to his eyeballs in HR grievances if he failed to adapt.

How our strengths become our weakness

I nudged Rohit to explore his strengths: his great resilience and drive for acceptance that had thrust him to the top of the sales leader board. He realised these strengths had become his biggest problem: he couldn't bear to see a lack of resilience or vulnerability in others because he'd had to bury these uncomfortable feelings himself. He was great at strategic conversations and dealing with facts. Anything deeper took him way beyond his comfort zone.

But he knew why and how he'd adapted to cope as a child. In coaching, once we realise where problems have developed, we can deal with the problem they create for us now. A therapeutic relationship is sometimes needed too, helping us make peace with our past if it holds us back today.

Listening, not telling, to build accountability

Once Rohit realised what he was doing, he began asking, not telling – getting people to talk through how they were doing and what they needed to improve. They were experienced enough to know the answers to their problems, they just needed space to think. Rohit added suggestions when they ran out of ideas, or if he could add real value from his own experience. People enjoyed the safe space he created for them, and he learned to be comfortable feeling vulnerable when people fell silent.

One of his team told me that Rohit had done a 180-degree shift from being a ranting dictator to a non-judgemental listening service.

My favourite question to most challenges . . .

Rohit asked his reports to talk through their performance and then asked this question: what's behind that?

I've had a great month. I hit my sales targets and won my biggest account ever.

What's behind that?

This question prods people to understand precisely what they did to create great sales, so they can repeat the pattern and success.

Ask this question *every time* someone explains any issue/ situation/challenge to you. It's tempting to dive into solving it for them, or try to make it better, or downplay it as *'it's not that bad'*. That's plain annoying and you could also be wrong. Just remember: 'There is a solution to every problem: simple, quick, and wrong' a quotation attributed to American journalist H.L. Mencken, novelist Mark Twain, and management guru and author Peter Drucker. Take your pick.

Ask *'what's behind that?'* and you are nudging the other person to identify and fix the problem – if that's possible. At the very least, you are listening for the extent of someone's awareness while you build a full picture. Sometimes we come up with solutions while thinking out loud.

The client won't return my calls.
What's behind that?
My wife isn't speaking to me.
What's behind that?
Our strategy isn't working.

What's behind that?

And so on. When someone runs out of useful answers, you need a follow-up question.

The blind-spot question: **What are you missing here?**

Ask this after someone has explored a situation and the reasons behind it, then appears to have run out of solutions. This uncovers their blind spots: the facts they don't yet know or haven't thought through.

Resources

BBC News (2023) Dominic Raab. See https://www.bbc.co.uk/news/uk-politics-65339102 (accessed 5 July 2024).

Vugt, M. von, Jepson, S.F., Hart, C.M. and de Cremer, D. (January 2004) Autocratic leadership in social dilemmas: a threat to group stability, *Journal of Experimental Social Psychology* 40(1): 1–13.

Chapter 6

How do I manage a cocky show-off?

'Dear Zena

I really dislike Harry, one lawyer in my team. I know
I shouldn't, but I do. He only does 'wow' pieces of work, leaving
all the boring, but essential, work to the rest of us. Of course, the
people in the business think he's great because he gives them
what they want. How do I manage him?'

Themes

- Trusted business partner
- Stakeholder management
- Prioritisation
- Time management

I come across a lot of Harry Hotshots, usually in middle to senior
roles. Their standard *modus operandi* when joining an organisation
is to start at a sprint, grasping no relevant context along the way.
They have rah-rah meetings with their teams, but don't listen to
what anyone says. Harry always knows best and thinks everyone
else is stupid. Very aware of the need to look good as fast as possible,
Harry launches a raft of showcase projects on top of existing
demands. Harry's team, already loaded to the limit, is pushed to the
edge.

By the time Harry's first year is up, someone further up the chain
likely gets suspicious, despite all of Harry's noise. They hear team
grumbles, spot accelerating staff attrition rates or the lack of results.
In complex corporate environments, it might be another six months
before Harry has left enough hard evidence for tough conversations
to start.

It may take another year before Harry moves on, so he's probably
certain of a safe two-year stint on LinkedIn. He knows how to

negotiate a decent pay-off while bagging a bigger job elsewhere because Harry knows how to talk a good game. Harrys are always careful to cultivate a head-hunter network, unlike less savvy colleagues who keep their heads down and get on with the job. The messaging that comes round is that Harry has moved on for a 'bigger challenge'.

Some Harrys pull this off multiple times in their careers. They are great at spinning their story. Hiring processes reward leadership competencies like 'confidence and impact' over 'reliable, consistent, cares about the customer', and choose Harry Hotshots instead of more self-effacing colleagues, the Steady Eddies.

This time, Harry wasn't one of those hotshots, he was just smart.

Harry was an in-house lawyer in a multinational food business working in the UK team, which looked after all European and Middle Eastern divisions. He reported to my client, Saira, the UK Head of Legal.

In-house lawyers aim to give sound counsel at the planning stages of a transaction, rather than carry out firefighting later on. Unlike more siloed functions like Sales or Finance, Legal should know what's going on across the business. This cross-functional knowledge allows them to join up the dots, giving them a valuable perspective. These are the people you want in all conversations, advising you of the best way to fulfil your plans. They should be trusted strategic advisors, not just a back-office transactional function.

That's the theory. In practice, anything involving a contract hits their inbox: paperwork for the new coffee machine or a standard sales agreement. If no one's being careful, in-house lawyers get mired in grunt work.

Lawyers usually start their careers working in law firms, where performance is measured on the number of billable hours racked up. It's in everyone's DNA to work long hours and keep clients happy. If they move in-house, they must unlearn this approach. Now, they need the quickest, most effective way to make the greatest impression on the people that really matter. If they do this well, they climb the career ladder and gain some life outside of work.

Harry had sussed this out. He was an expert at building relationships, spending time with his important business stakeholders to grasp what mattered most to them: their 'key drivers'. They called him for advice, sometimes just for a chat about what they were up to. Harry was brilliant at execution. He knew the right time to slow transactions, when he needed more views. When he acted, he got things right instantly.

This Hotshot Harry was a poster-boy for being a fully-blown strategic advisor. Anyone could see he had a stellar career ahead, perhaps staying in legal or maybe leveraging his relationships to move into business operations.

Back in the trenches, Saira and her team were working super hard and felt that they weren't being appreciated. They felt bitter. We unpacked all of this in our conversations.

Harry was getting all the glory. The rest of them were keeping the show on the road and, in Saira's words, 'stopping the business from going over a cliff'. They were doing the unsexy, but essential, legal demands that no one cared about because they didn't really understand what a legal function really does.

Saira admitted she was annoyed with Harry only because he was a reminder of where she felt she was going wrong. If people in the business did a Who's Who of the legal department, they might even assume Harry was at the top of the tree. He showed more executive presence and commercial clout than she did. Saira needed to flex her leadership muscles and recalibrate how and where the team operated. She was an impressive lawyer; it was time for her to lean in on the leadership part of her job.

Instead of moaning about Harry, what could the rest of the team learn from him? He wasn't doing a land grab, taking responsibility or credit from them. All he was guilty of was ruthless prioritisation. Saira needed to encourage everyone to adopt the same approach, making sure everyone also did their share of routine grunt work.

Saira stepped up. She took her team away for a couple of days, for what she called a Hard Reset, an event I was fortunate in facilitating. The theme was: What do we stand for and how can we excel at it?

The structure was:

1 **Clarity. What do we bring to the table?**
The team discussed their purpose and value, coming up with easy messaging that their stakeholders would grasp easily. What's our contribution and why should it matter to you? This unifying sense of purpose had two benefits. It improved the internal branding and respect for the legal function, and a new sense of belonging improved the culture and team retention rates.

2 **Priorities. How should we spend our time to achieve this purpose?**
They delved into the nuts and bolts of how they worked. If they wanted time to build relationships and have more strategic conversations, what had to change? How could they make contract execution more efficient and straightforward?

We discovered some of the team wasted time on clauses that didn't matter. Harry explained how he quickly got to what highly experienced in-house lawyer Jamie Pearson calls the 'signature moment', even in complicated high-risk contract negotiations. Someone confessed to spending hours on pristine formatting, in pursuit of a perfect document. Harry was a generous and supportive colleague during the discussions, but I enjoyed watching him trying not to laugh at this – Harry wasn't the least bit bothered about straight lines.

Was Harry a problem hotshot? No, this Harry was a fantastic asset and Saira realised it. He kept her on her toes, made the whole team raise their game and the high regard he'd racked up made her look good, too. Rather than crushing him or letting him get bored – he'd have been a flight risk if she'd done this – she pushed him to do more. He took part in global legal meetings and represented the company about legislative changes at consumer industry forums.

In my last session with her, Saira thought about whether it was time to give Harry people to manage directly and how she could support him doing this.

These are the questions to ask yourself if someone annoys you – and be honest:

- Why does this person wind me up so much?
- Could they remind me of myself?

Resources

Jamie Pearson and Sarah Marshall's excellent career development series for in-house lawyers, Sarah & Jamie's HIGH FIVE. See https://sarahjamie.substack.com (accessed 5 July 2024).

Chapter 7

I'm doing my team's work as well as my own

'Dear Zena

I manage a young, busy procurement team who seems to do the minimum asked of them, but no more. They complain if I ask them to do extra, as if it's a big favour. I end up picking up the slack on top of my normal workload. When they grudgingly appear in the office, they have their coats on by 5.30. I'm knackered and resentful. How do I get them to grow up and step up?'

Themes

- Accidental managers
- Parent/Adult model of transactional analysis
- Rescuers and over-nurturing managers
- Co-dependence
- Accountability

This dilemma might seem like a stereotypical case of a work-shy, entitled Gen-Z team: they don't want to work, but expect a lot without giving much . . . I could go on.

But I'm not keen on lumping groups together and I don't agree with the stereotype. The Gen-Z cohort might demand more meaning from their work, but what's wrong with that? In my experience, they prize autonomy and balance. They may not want to give their employer their devotion, but they still expect work to have a sense of purpose and to align with their values. They want their employer to develop their talents in return for contributing their time and skills. Sounds reasonable to me.

This team's problematic behaviour was caused by their manager's problematic behaviour. When he changed his behaviour, they changed theirs.

The rescuer manager

The stereotypical terrible boss is an insensitive bully. Word soon gets round about them and, thankfully, they are a dying breed. Harder to spot is another bad boss, the smothering rescuer or mother-hen manager. These are caring, conscientious people but feeble managers.

Kumar was a procurement lead in his early 30s. He had fallen into the rescuing trap when he first took over the team. He wanted to be the best boss he'd never had.

His interpretation of a manager's role was like being the team's dad: a kind, patriarchal head of the family, there to keep everyone stress-free and happy. When he first started managing, he felt guilty if anyone in his team said they were feeling a tad overwhelmed. Instead of helping them prioritise their work, he did it for them. It was the line of least resistance, and no one learned anything new.

Kumar's own line manager, Kush, was in a different time zone, so he wasn't much of a role model. Kush hadn't heard of problems via the grapevine, and the work was getting done on time and to a professional standard: why would he imagine any problems rumbling away under the surface? Kumar didn't like to admit that he was struggling.

The transition from individual team member to manager can be tricky. Kumar previously had little support in how to manage or how much of his time he should spend supporting others.

The UK's Chartered Institute of Management estimates that 82 per cent of workers moving into management roles are accidental managers like Kumar, making it up as they go. Young people who most need management supervision are working for untrained managers who don't know how to give it.

Management performance systems often mask people like Kumar because his team gave him adequate scores. They didn't want to hurt his feelings; he was a lovely guy after all, but hopeless.

Leaving the mummy in the museum

Kumar's team didn't need him to backfill for them. They needed him to step up and manage the team. They needed guidance and clarity on the structure of their roles, they needed him to spell out the standards and objectives expected of them and they needed to learn how to negotiate the scope of their projects with other teams and learn to ask for help when necessary. And they wanted coaching and career development.

All of this came to light when an alert HR director did some discreet digging and saw some familiar patterns. Kumar's nurturing style was frustrating high-potential staff who wanted to be challenged, not mollycoddled. His distaste for 'difficult' conversations meant Kumar sugar-coated feedback to the point where people had no idea where and how they could improve or develop. They wanted to move on quickly. Other team members simply took advantage of Kumar's kind nature.

One leaver described working for him as a break at motorway services on a long car journey. It was pleasant, but everyone knew they couldn't stay there long.

In our first coaching session, I asked Kumar about the consequences of him continuing to work like this. He admitted to being fed up. He'd cancelled his gym membership and dating apps because he was too busy with work. He was thinking of applying for roles without management responsibility so he could get his life back. The job title wasn't worth the aggro. But he also realised that was a self-sabotaging approach, the wrong way to handle his problem.

I needed to show that his behaviour was the cause. His team was subconsciously responding to him and not in a healthy, professional way. Here's the model I used. I give it a lot of space because once you understand the model, you'll spot the dynamics everywhere you look, especially between children and parents. It's transformative.

The parent–adult–child model of transactional analysis

Dr Eric Berne, a Canadian-born psychiatrist, created a theory of transactional analysis as a way of explaining our behaviour in different situations, or 'transactions', depending on the behaviour of other people. Our brains have three distinct ego states: parent, adult and child.

The parent ego state emerges from the rules and values we learned from our parents or authority figures. The adult ego state is based on rational thinking and problem-solving, appropriate to what's in front of us right now. The child ego state is driven by emotions, impulses and needs.

(P)	Parent ego state
	Responses copied from our parents/parent figures can nurture or criticise. The nurturing ego style is useful when we need to be a hero or extra supportive. The critical parent ego style can control and dominate, urging us to belittle others and have favourites.
(A)	Adult ego state
	The adult state generates logical, stable and consistent behaviour, where we rationally process our thoughts and behaviour based on facts. This is appropriate for our professional job roles. In the workplace, this is the ego state we should be in most of the time.
(C)	Child ego state
	Responses in this ego state emerge from our childhood and can be playful or defensive. Being a playful, curious, adventurous child is brilliant when you need to be creative, as long as we return to a more rational adult ego state at an appropriate time.

Unhealthy transactions

The parent–adult–child model helps us to understand workplace conflict and why we behave in contrasting ways with different people. Grasping this helps us to improve our relationships and build more positive cultures because we understand where unhealthy conflict shows up. It's a reassuring model, demonstrating how other people respond inappropriately and even weirdly in different situations; it's not just us. Why do we feel awkward around some people or intolerant of others?

There's a place for each of the ego states. Even the critical parent ego state is useful in a crisis or situation where an expert is needed, although these are often the start of bad behaviour. This can also be a dangerous state too, as a critical parent may think they know best and ignore facts that suggest the opposite – like a doctor who ignores a patient's concerns.

Watch any true crime programmes that feature an old-school police officer with a 'seen-it-all-before' critical parent attitude. They'll look for evidence to convict a person they assume is a murderer – usually a husband or bad mother – ignoring signs and proof that someone else is the actual killer.

Critical parents who are unnecessarily personal in their feedback – or plain shouty – easily shift us out of our adult ego state into a critical, shouty parent to match theirs. Anyone in a customer service role can relate to this. They learn to work hard to stay grounded in a professional, calm and adult ego state.

When someone pauses and lowers their voice, an angry person usually does the same. We may equally go into a defensive child ego state, with a flight, freeze or fawn response, depending on how we coped with conflict as a child.

Imagine you ask for feedback on a piece of work. Your manager is in critical parent and says something like: '*you keep making careless mistakes.*'

This pushes you from an adult to a defensive child state, where you feel resentful and annoyed, maybe rebellious and over-sensitive. You withhold your ideas and don't ask for feedback again.

If your manager had stayed in adult and said something more empowering: *'I've definitely seen a couple of mistakes in the report, let's figure out what's going on here',* you'd have likely stayed in constructive, professional adult too.

In Kumar's case, he had moved from adult ego state to mostly nurturing parent. Then he switched to passive-aggressive child when he felt hard done by and resentful. In response, most of his team had slid into child – and stayed there.

Sometimes they were in a playful child ego state – not doing their work, being late for meetings and missing deadlines. It was as if they were pushing to see what they could get away with. Or they were defensive, doing the bare minimum of work, or looking to move internally or externally, without explaining to Kumar what they needed from him. They were just throwing their toys out of the pram, not looking for or not finding a professional solution.

The adult ego state is the one that allows us to express our needs and opinions professionally, without being aggressive or passive. It creates fruitful, productive relationships with healthy friction. That's where Kumar and all his team needed to be.

This might sound like hippy-dippy indulgence, but it really works. I've worked with many organisations who had the same problems as Kumar post-pandemic. Leaders had shifted into hero, nurturing adult during lockdowns, taking responsibility for everyone's well-being, then luring them back into the office with croissants and fun activities. Six months later, they noticed employees still expected their employer to solve problems for them. When the leaders returned to an adult ego state – their professional roles – clarifying the normal structure, purpose and roles, their teams stepped up and took more accountability.

Kumar loved this model. We talked at length about what stepping into an adult ego state meant in practice and what steps he could take to stay in that lane. If he was in adult, people really would meet him there.

Kumar called a team meeting and communicated far more confidently with them than he had done before. He explained he wanted to refresh the way the team worked. He outlined the critical demands the team faced and asked *them* how they thought they could meet them.

Normally, he'd have presented a ready-made plan. It took a few awkward rounds, asking each person what they thought, but it brought up plenty of ideas and solutions which were mostly acted upon.

Kumar had to work hard to bring people up to higher, more challenging standards. He gained confidence in giving feedback on the hoof, and I trained him on how to coach in his one-to-one feedback sessions. He had to put up guard rails around his adult ego state to remain at this professional level, especially when he felt under pressure.

In the past, if someone had sent Kumar half-completed work, he would have filled the gaps as the quickest, easiest option. The new Kumar had learned to return unfinished work, explaining what that person needed to finish by a clear deadline.

As Kumar showed his team more respect for their ability to manage their workload and carry out work to a professional standard, he earned their respect.

A final word about Kumar. When we met, he was already a lovely, compassionate person. When I caught up with him some time later, he told me that the dating apps he'd thought of ditching worked and that he was channelling his rescuing tendencies in a much more boundaried way. He and his lovely partner had adopted two Bernese mountain dogs.

Co-dependence

Kumar's nurturing parent behaviour likely has an element of co-dependence behind it.

Co-dependency is an unhealthy relationship where one person tolerates or even enables another's destructive, self-sabotaging behaviour. Family relationships with addicts first brought this to light in situations where co-dependent family members covered up, or even facilitated, the addiction. This can lead to rescuing behaviour in other relationships, including in the workplace.

Co-dependent people learn early in life that they are responsible for everyone else and it is their job to keep the show on the road. They are great employees because they work harder than everyone else. They may have been too attentive to their parents' feelings and needs, rather than their parents being attuned to theirs. As a result, the co-dependent person's self-worth is tied up in this over-functioning behaviour.

You can sense their fragility and lack of boundaries. Exhausted, they are often snappy and on a short fuse, putting a ceiling on their career prospects. They find it hard to stand up for themselves.

A warning sign of co-dependent behaviour is when people are terrified of upsetting others. They won't say no or state their own needs if that goes against what the other person might want. It's a reason why some managers struggle to give developmental feedback or bad news.

Resources

Beattie, M. (1986) *Codependent No More: How to Stop Controlling Others and Start Caring for Yourself,* Hazelden Publishing.

CMI (online) Taking responsibility – why UK PLC needs better managers. See: https://www.managers.org.uk/wp-content/uploads/2023/10/CMI_BMB_GoodManagment_Report.pdf (accessed 8 July 2024).

Harris, T.A. (2012) *I'm Ok, You're OK: A Practical Approach to Human Psychology,* Arrow.

Stewart, I. and Joines, V. (2012) *T A Today: A New Introduction to Transactional Analysis,* Lifespace Publishing.

Chapter 8

My star performer is underperforming

'Dear Zena

I used to trust Ellie to do a great job but, now she's working from home, she doesn't seem to do much work at all. Why has her performance slipped? Is she lazy? Is she leaving? What's going on?'

Themes

- Parkinson's law and time management
- People-pleasing
- Laissez-faire leaders
- Discretionary activities and employee resource groups
- Efficiency and productivity

Operation director Curtis had this problem when he was on one of my leadership programmes. Ellie, one of his team members, was a couple of years out of university. She used to be an ambitious ball of energy, a superstar, one with a reputation for getting things done.

During the past few months, her productivity had tailed off. She met deadlines, but Curtis had feedback that her work was rushed and barely good enough. Curtis instinctively looked on the dark side, so his immediate conclusion was that Ellie's heart was no longer in the job. Maybe she was looking for another job? Ellie worked mostly from home, so it was hard to assess what she did all day. She seemed responsive to messages and emails and showed up promptly, camera on, at meetings. It was what she did the rest of the day that was a mystery, and the problem he faced.

In 1955 British naval historian and author Cyril Northcote Parkinson wrote a great opening line for an article in *The Economist*: 'Work expands so as to fill the time available for its completion'. He was complaining about the inefficiencies of the British Civil

Service and used the example of an elderly lady writing a postcard to her niece. She had nothing else to do, so buying exactly the right card, writing the perfect message and then heading out to post the card consumed her entire day.

Perhaps Parkinson's law could explain what was going on with Ellie? Was she stretching out tasks to fill the day and putting in minimum effort? Did she need more tasks, more deadlines, more challenging work? Sometimes when performance has tailed off, people need an interesting side-project to get their motivation back. Should Curtis lean on her a bit more?

But wait, slow down a bit. The obvious answer to any people problem is usually the wrong one. Not so long ago, Ellie was an ambitious and eager-to-please top performer.

Curtis met with Ellie and asked what she was working on. Gentle probing showed she was a victim of her own success. She did such a great job, she was now contributing more than her fair share in the team. She was also involved in some cross-team projects Curtis was unaware of; other managers had sneakily gone directly to Ellie without telling him. She hadn't wanted to flag up how much work she had, but she didn't have enough week at the end of her work. Sometimes she had no clue where to start, so she stayed stuck, triaging emails.

What happens when we are overwhelmed?

Dr Sheena Iyengar of Columbia University Business School did an intriguing experiment to show how having too much choice overwhelms us to the point of rendering us incapable of making decisions. People were taken to a shopping mall and offered samples of six varieties of jam available to buy, while another group was presented with 24 jam options. The six-jam group was ten times more likely to buy a jam because they weren't lost in a fog of overwhelm. It's like the feisty TV programmes where celebrated

UK chef Gordon Ramsay regularly screamed at restauranteurs to simplify their fancy menus because customers simply had too much choice.

What has this to do with us? When people have too much to do, they become overwhelmed. Easy red flags will help you spot this. You'll notice reduced output and more 'busy work': emails, messages and low-value tasks, rather than meeting key deadlines. When we are wired and tired, it is hard to separate what's important, our real priorities and what some chaotic colleague has made urgent because they fail to plan properly. It's the urgency effect: to keep us safe, we respond to what's screaming in front of us. Only now we are reacting to Teams notifications, not woolly mammoths bearing down on us. We chase our tails, achieving little of value.

Curtis worked with Ellie to take some of the jam off her table. He helped her to prioritise and taught her to push back. When people wanted her to do something, she asked: 'When is the latest you need this by?'

This helped her better manage her diary, so she felt back in control. Most work deadlines are arbitrary and it's easier than you might think to sequence tasks to suit, rather than have everything land on you at once.

Ellie grew used to saying: *'I can do it when I've got this planning signed off, so I can start this by next Tuesday. Is that okay?'*

Or: *'I can do it, but I'll have to delay this report I'm working on for a couple of days. Is that OK?'*

Sometimes, she'd say a friendly but firm no.

'I'd love to get involved with your project, but I don't have the time to do it justice.'

'I'd love to help, but I'm drowning in these priorities this month.'

Reframing

Curtis coached Ellie on her core beliefs, replacing the high-pressure demands she put on herself with more realistic, kinder beliefs.

'What are you demanding of yourself? What are you telling yourself?'

I'm sure you've already worked out that Ellie put pressure on herself to be a high achiever, keeping everyone happy.

Curtis helped her reframe this to be kinder to herself.

'Is it possible to please everyone all the time?'

'Is it realistic to always work harder than everyone else?'

'What's better – to work smart or work hard?'

As Ellie discovered, long hours simply don't equate to better work and there are no prizes for being nice, carrying out everyone else's priorities other than your own.

Curtis gets a grip on his role

Even the most efficient of us can hit a wall with too much to do. This was a wake-up call for Curtis. I was teaching him to coach and build accountability within his team, but he couldn't start doing this until everyone was established in the right role, doing the right tasks, equipped with the right skills.

I asked why Ellie hadn't come to him for help and how he'd let the problem get this far. He'd become used to asking people how they were, taking their 'fine thanks' answers at face value. It was a relief to Curtis since he was busy, too.

He realised he had been guilty of letting Ellie get on with things because he didn't want to be seen as a micro-manager. But he had gone too far in the other direction. He was what Professor of Psychology at Stanford University, Geoffrey L. Cohen, calls a 'laissez-faire' manager. The rest of us would probably call it being useless. He had become overly hands-off and wasn't aware of who was doing what in his team. In case you're wondering, laissez-faire leaders are as ineffective as old-school autocratic ones.

Curtis's team needed him to get more involved in the granular details of what everyone did each day. He discovered at least another team member was stressed by their workload, while a couple weren't pulling their weight.

Curtis needed to get a firm grip on managing his team's workflow. That's not micro-management; that's the job. Managers have an ethical responsibility to make sure that tasks fit the time available to do them – the hours people are paid to work. Home working and 24/7 communication have pushed the boundaries between work time and personal time, so people often cannibalise their own time to squeeze everything in.

Focusing on 'busy work' during long hours is never the way to productivity; it's an obstacle to it.

Curtis was responsible for the output of his team and had to make it as easy as possible for them to get work done in reasonable working hours. It's okay to get granular with employees when they are stressed to discover what they've got on their plate. Are they over-committing to work, or finessing things that don't need perfection: writing a lengthy report instead of nailing a few bullet points or fiddling with a PowerPoint deck, a common time-suck? This often happens with people who want everything to be perfect.

Curtis introduced an old-school, daily kick-off meeting, a time when everyone talked through their priorities and when they'd tackle them.

He spoke to his peers in the organisation to discover why his team was being pulled onto other projects. Getting involved in curveballs like this can be a useful career opportunity, providing access to new networks and knowledge. At other times, it's simply extra work covering up for staff shortages. The result is a casualty like Ellie who ends up doing too much. Successful people are better at saying no when they can't see any personal upside from getting pulled into curveballs. They are less worried about upsetting people and don't feel responsible for everyone else's problems.

Useful questions to help someone feel less overwhelmed

Can you walk me through your priorities?
When is the latest you need this by? (When someone wants you to do something.)

When is the earliest you can do it? (When you want someone to do something for you.)

If you say yes to this, what will you say no to?

What's my purpose? What am I trying to achieve? Who do I really want to help?

A warning about taking on too much

One way HR departments judge the engagement of their workforce is by measuring discretionary effort. This describes how people get involved above and beyond their regular performance expectation and go the extra mile.

Discretionary effort is seen as evidence of a motivated and cheery culture, perhaps payback for establishing it. This includes employees making a call to a customer to check they are happy, mentoring others, volunteering, making suggestions or training others. It's especially valued with frontline employees and leads to higher sales, better customer satisfaction, repeat business and that holy grail – greater shareholder value.

What was once picking up litter and making a few extra phones calls has morphed into commitment to bigger initiatives. Employee Resource Groups (ERGs) are an example – not to be confused with the UK's right-wing European Research Group in the Conservative political party. ERGs are groups of employees who share characteristics or life experiences and join to support each other. Usually these are fantastic groups that offer a chance to build connections and networks.

But, there's a but . . . My aim is to help people be happy and productive within reasonable working hours, then to switch off, recharge their energy and have a fulfilling life across all measures.

I've lost count of the people I've met who are drowning with their workload yet are extensively involved in networking groups or similar discretionary activities. They get involved because they enjoy them and flourish with the social connection, but sometimes feel they should be seen to participate. High-achieving people-pleasers like Ellie are vulnerable to this because they are the dynamic people everyone wants onboard – and they're dreadful at saying no. They end up working all hours trying to handle everything and keep everyone happy.

It's not career enhancing to struggle on areas where you're being judged, thanks to the time you spend on other activities. I've coached one client who ran a vibrant women's network in her bank, only for the promotion that should have been hers to go to a man with less experience. He'd simply been more visibly effective in the core job role. Ouch!

Be smart about your time and energy

I'm not saying don't get involved, just be smart about it. Be judicious with the trade-off with your time. If you do these things, go large and make a big deal of it. Corporate life rewards visibility, not unsung heroes. Get some buy-in from your senior stakeholders and plaster it over your LinkedIn profile so people can see what you stand for.

You can't invent extra time: what must go? Perhaps you can delegate some of the less valuable tasks you do, to create some room in your calendar.

As Curtis asked Ellie: *'If you say yes to this, what must you say no to?'*

Remind yourself of your priorities.

'What are your goals? What are you trying to achieve? Who are you aiming to serve?'

This extra activity or side project might get you there more effectively than the day job, so decide what you want from it and how you'll make it happen.

Resources

Cohen, G.L. (2022) *Belonging: The Science of Creating Connection and Bridging Divides*, W. W. Norton & Company.

Iyengar, S. (2011) *The Art of Choosing: The Decisions We Make Every day of our Lives, What They Say About Us and How We Can Improve Them,* Abacus.

Northcote Parkinson, C. (1955) Letter to the *Economist*, reprinted July 2020. See https://www.economist.com/news/1955/11/19/parkinsons-law (accessed 8 July 2024).

Chapter 9

How do I ignite a demotivated team?

- -

'Dear Zena

My new team is apathetic and complacent. Everyone seems to be cynically going through the motions. I don't think they are lazy; some seem to have more to offer but just aren't interested in stepping up. But they've definitely lost motivation. How do I put a rocket up them?'

- -

Themes

- Motivation
- Purpose
- Visioning skills
- Trust and psychological safety

When my client Sandra joined the London team of a global PR agency, she was enthusiastically onboarded, even given a high-priced swag-bag of cool products her firm represented.

She soon found herself disappointed to discover that the razzmatazz elsewhere in the business was offset by the lacklustre mood of her new team. None was uncooperative, but they all seemed to plod with little interest, let alone passion or enthusiasm.

They lacked faith in the business's leadership and appeared cynical about the service they were offering to clients. They were friendly to Sandra, but with a tired 'we've seen all these new things before, but they won't work' vibe. No one had told Sandra any of this during her interview, but neither had she asked specific questions about team performance.

What should Sandra do? Bail? She had other job offers she could easily take up. Or should she fire them all and bring in her own people?

Fortunately, Sandra took neither of these slightly extreme options. She was experienced enough to spot a team with potential that needed igniting. The question was simple: how?

She learned the team had gone through two directors in less than two years, both of whom had been more interested in their own profiles than supporting and developing the team. There was no cohesive system or support when some clients became too demanding.

None of the team seemed a flight risk. They acted as if they had a job for life. They had above-average salaries and decent levels of flexibility, so they were doing okay. But that was it. Okay was about as much support as they were getting from work and they were giving an okay performance in return.

Sandra was savvy enough to grasp that the underlying problem wasn't performance management or ensuring that she had the right people in the right roles. Those were important issues and would come later. First, her team needed a sense of purpose. They needed to be inspired.

A purpose is not getting a pay rise; purpose is something bigger than you

As bestselling author Simon Sinek says in *Start with Why,* great companies don't hire skilled people and motivate them, they hire already motivated people and inspire them. They inspire them by giving them something bigger than their job to work towards.

I have a friend we'll call Amanda who works in the UK Parliament; she's had a successful career in publishing and still writes at home on her own projects. But she wanted a part-time role that offered exercise – writing being a sedentary job – and varied contact with people.

At the UK Parliament, Amanda has a low-paid role where she carries out tours of the estate. Some of these can be booked through members of parliament and are aimed at encouraging democratic engagement. Others are commercial tours and attract overseas visitors. She helps visitors to lobby their MP, watches debates in the public galleries, guides visitors with mobility issues to events, or sometimes to committee rooms where they may give evidence or watch proceedings. It's a large, Victorian building, retrofitted to make sure mobility cannot stop democratic access.

On the surface, it sounded a strange career move, so I asked the obvious question: why?

'I wanted something with purpose,' she said, 'and working in the seat of our democracy offers purpose on steroids. Delivering a tour about how our democracy has developed . . . helping people into the galleries or to lobby their MP . . . showing them how they can do much more than vote . . . pretty much everything in the job has democracy as a touchstone. MPs and peers can be delightful or "entitled". And the same goes for their staff. But no job is perfect.'

What about the protests and demonstrations? The tight security? 'Working at the Houses of Parliament has undeniable concerns; the demonstrations are regular, noisy and have to be managed with care,' said Amanda. 'But I love them; they take me back to my rebellious student days and reassure me I'm not living in North Korea.'

Work at the UK Parliament carries a strong, baked-in purpose. It may be harder to find elsewhere, especially if a team is dispirited and cynical.

Wayne Rooney, one of England's golden generation of footballers, was sacked by Birmingham City after only 83 days as manager. Steven Gerrard and Frank Lampard, once lauded as players, went through turbulent times as Premier League managers. Other fellow star players also failed to make a lasting impact.

Heroes on the field, but lacklustre as managers, while players from other countries made a seamless transition. Why?

Jonathan Liew of *The New Statesman* attributes it to having a defined, shared identity – or for Rooney and friends the lack of identity.

The successful French team of 1998–2000 were renowned for their technical ability; the Spanish team of 2008–2010 perfected the passing game. The English players moved into management without having learned to establish a strong sense of connection. As players, they had celebrity, ego and great clothes; they needed more to become great managers.

Strong culture and a shared purpose matters.

So when someone tells me they aren't happy at work, or they feel stuck, I check for three things.

1 **Intellectual challenge** – is the team bored? Is the work stimulating enough, and are the team members learning?

2 **Control** – do employees have enough mastery over which tasks they do, as well as where, when and how they do them? Within reason, of course.

These two can normally be fixed easily. The third issue is the deal-breaker.

3 **Values and purpose** – This is the crucial 'something bigger' element. Do the beliefs and values of team members align with the culture in which they work? Do they know why the organisation exists and do they back that purpose? Do they share the same beliefs and world view as the people they work with?

If there is a disconnect in values, people might hang on a bit for their own personal reasons, but they will soon move on to a culture that inspires them and gives them a reason for getting up in the morning. Something other than getting paid.

Visioning techniques

I worked with Sandra on arousing her team around a strong sense of purpose.

Sandra put the building blocks in place first, spending time with everyone to ensure that the right person was in the right job while clarifying role and performance needs where necessary. Then she took everyone away for a day to work out what they stood for.

Deborah Ancona is the Seley Distinguished Professor of Management at the MIT Sloan School of Management and the founder and faculty director of the MIT Leadership Center. She has a framework of four key leadership capabilities: sensemaking, relating, visioning and inventing. Visioning is creating an image of what can be possible, and this is what Sandra did with her team.

Many years ago, I was taught the old-school sales technique of first finding out what the buyer's problem is and then selling a solution to that problem. You probably know the patter: 'Woah, your old fountain pen leaks? You need to buy this shiny one which won't get ink all over your fingers.'

Solving a problem this way might land a sale and it can be a useful technique in coaching too, getting people to list in detail all the problems with their current situation so they accept the need to change.

Sandra needed to inspire hearts and minds, so she had to flip this approach.

She took the team straight to imagining what difference it would make if everything was going brilliantly, rather than everyone getting bogged down by coping with the daily grind.

Who are we and *who do we want to become?* These are standard questions in this context, but we've all sat through tedious mission-statement presentations that ask this. And they're often no more than lip service too. You need questions that lift people's thinking up to a more inspirational level. Sandra's people also needed a bit of edge, some safe but healthy friction in the team to liven them up.

She took her team straight to the sunny uplands, by using magic questions to raise their thinking to what was possible.

The magic question: imagine if . . .

Here are the kind of questions she asked to spark up their thinking.

'Imagine if our clients were delighted with us . . . what difference would that make to how we worked?'

'Imagine if our clients were so loyal that we never had to worry about losing them . . . what difference would that make to the creative risks we could offer them?'

'Imagine if we won the Agency of the Year Award . . . what difference would that make to our confidence?'

'Imagine if we could win more ambitious creative clients . . . what could we do differently?'

'Imagine if our client relationships improved . . . what would we notice?'

These questions shift people from the daily grind to thinking about why they do what they do. You ask a mix of questions until you hit the one that gets people painting a picture of what is possible. It can take considerable time, especially when people aren't used to this type of group work, but once one person gets it, the others join in. Only when all ideas have dried up – and some people will surprise you with their creativity – do you then discuss the practicalities of each suggestion.

Inspiring purpose like this is the hallmark of outstanding leaders who build high-performing, happy teams. We've all heard the cheesy story of the tired worker who is laying bricks vs the inspired one who is building a cathedral. Creative brainstorming like this gives space for people to mention opportunities and ideas that reach beyond the daily grind, maybe generating the one big idea that creates a huge competitive advantage. Throw in a magic question into team meetings to encourage this creativity and get people to speak up.

Sandra created a crucial safe space

I trust you never respond to any idea with sarcasm or eye-rolling. That should always be the case, but you'll lose trust forever if you slap people and their ideas down in a public forum where people are out of their comfort zone. I have seen senior leaders shut down people in these types of meetings, particularly when they see comments as personal criticism or the chance of extra work coming their way because of another person's suggestion.

Amy Edmondson is the Novartis Professor of Leadership and Management at the Harvard Business School. I mentioned her concept of psychological safety in my introduction because it is vital to building trust and elevating performance, which is exactly what Sandra needed to do.

Edmondson wrote that businesses in our modern economic world depend on a persistent flow of new ideas and critical thought, so organisations have to create a space where employees can voice their thoughts and opinions without fear of ridicule or worse.

Her research in her 2019 book *The Fearless Organisation, Creating Psychological Safety in the Workplace* showed that 30 per cent of people across a range of industries stay silent from fear of being labelled a troublemaker. Twenty-five per cent thought speaking up would make no impact whatsoever, and 22.5 per cent were concerned they'd lose their jobs if they spoke up.

When I ask managers if they have been trained in psychological safety, they often say, yes, of course they are: 'We really care. We look after everyone; if anything we spoon-feed them'. They are misunderstanding the idea of psychological safety. As we'll repeatedly see, it's about being safe to speak up and challenge, without fear of repercussions.

If you want to discover the level of psychological safety in your teams, then ask them this direct question: 'Do you feel your manager has your back?'

At my first job in a recruitment agency, I was sent to head office for training with two other relative newbies. When we returned to our office, our manager was literally waiting at the door, ready to berate us for 'admitting there were things you didn't know'. 'Never, ever, do that again', she declared, clearly having already been told off because of gaps in our knowledge.

We were only two weeks into our jobs, but the bubble had burst for good. The firm spent a fortune on glitzy incentives for us, but you can't buy trust. We hit the targets we were given, but that was all our manager got out of us. Why should we line her pockets?

No loyalty. No trust. No extra mile. We never volunteered ideas for better client service, and we didn't stay for long. If you want a productive team, you need to do the exact opposite of this. Your people must feel safe to be vulnerable: to admit what they don't know, speak up about problems, challenge the status quo, spot opportunities and come up with ideas.

You need people to step out of their comfort zone and trust they won't be punished for making mistakes. The people at the coalface are the ones who spot problems and raise performance, and they must feel empowered to do this. They shouldn't wait to be asked. Some friction is fine and is probably to be encouraged, provided trust has been built first.

Successful leaders create trust and respect. Psychologists have identified 'conversational turn-taking' and 'social sensitivity' as important aspects in creating psychological safety.

Building trust in a brainstorm

Sandra kept going round the table for ideas, writing them on a whiteboard, never criticising, just encouraging. This wasn't a performance management exercise or a skills assessment; she was getting people to come up with collective goals that inspired everyone.

She was also showing the team it was safe to speak up and be brave in their thinking. Not everyone loved it, of course; you'll never please everyone, but the better performers embraced the process.

Tips for building a culture of psychological safety

1 **Open communication channels.** Stay tuned to your team's progress with regular check-ins – not check-ups – so people know you will listen to them if they have a problem. Ask 'how's it going with X' and actively listen to what people say. You may get a 'it's fine' comment, so ask a follow-up. Prod gently for more.

➤

2 **Never mock or be cynical.** Genuinely encourage ideas and never criticise quirky contributions in meetings or allow it from team members. Sarcastic comments like 'that's certainly one idea, any others?' get cheap laughs but shut down creativity and trust. Be open to ideas that don't match your own.

3 **Set a meeting etiquette.** Meetings are where psychological safety is really on display. Set respectful boundaries – everyone's voice is heard, and we look at the person speaking. Even if we are all online, we don't interrupt each other.

4 **Deal with problems head on.** Don't shy away from bad news, surface tensions and disagreements. Dig for as much accurate information as possible, analyse the causes, fix the problem and collectively change the process. Show the team how to learn from failure and look for lessons. Our best times at work are when we are overcoming challenges and learning how to do better.

5 **Don't get personal and keep it all about work.** Don't have favourites, share gossip or be overtly political. Focus on the delivery of work to the highest possible standards and people's contribution. Be objective. Give feedback on behaviours and performance, not traits – more about this in the next chapter. If you've been promoted and are now managing friends, have a grown-up conversation about how you will navigate boundaries with them so you can all flourish professionally.

6 **Acknowledge your own mistakes and vulnerabilities.** Lead by example – as always. You too are fallible and accept you aren't supposed to know everything. Ask questions you also want the team to ask each other.

> 'Can you double-check the facts for me; I don't want to miss anything?'
>
> 'What am I not seeing now that will be obvious when I'm at the end of the project?'
>
> 'What are my blind spots on this?'
>
> 'Am I getting in the way here?'
>
> 'What do you need from me now, and where can I back off?'
>
> 'How do you want to work together on this?'

Resources

Ancona, D. and Bresman, H. (updated edition, 2023) *X-Teams: How to Build Teams That Lead, Innovate, and Succeed,* Harvard Business Review Press.

Edmondson, A.C. (2018) *The Fearless Organization, Creating Psychological Safety in the Workplace,* Wiley.

Sinek, S. (2011) *Start with Why,* Wiley.

The New Statesman (online) See: https://www.newstatesman.com/culture/sport/2022/10/englands-golden-generation-failed-football-managers (accessed 8 July 2024).

Chapter 10

I'm too busy with no time to think

'Dear Zena

I've been hired as creative director, but I can't remember the last time I had time to think about anything, never mind come up with any creative ideas. Despite my best intentions, I'm totally bogged down in the weeds, playing Whac-a-Mole with constant demands. I can't prioritise and I've no time for my team. I'm worried I might get fired at this rate. It's not sustainable to keep going like this – I'll crash and burn.'

> ## Themes
>
> - Deep, flow working
> - Time management
> - Synchronous and asynchronous working

In 1913, a group of avant-garde artists in London rebelled against genteel, romantic British traditional art; instead, they celebrated the energy and dynamism of the modern machine age. Calling their art *Vorticism*, they used an abstract style with bright colours, sharp angles and hard lines to depict the movement of industrial life.

The vortex was an image of the creative energy swirling around and within the group, but the point of their art was the quiet, creative space found in the middle of the vortex. Founder of the movement Wyndham Lewis described it as a great silent place in the whirlpool's heart where all the energy was concentrated.

That great silent place is what's missing in today's digital machine age. My client Joachim, ten months into a job in an advertising and communications firm, was a perfect example of this problem. His day was a busy whirl, with no time or space for quiet creativity in the middle.

I asked Joachim about the contribution he was supposed to make – his *highest and best use*. Why was he hired? His job was to engage with clients and lead and motivate his team, but most of all, to come up with exciting creative ideas. The quality of his thinking was why his team wanted to work for him and why their clients wanted him to run their accounts. And it was why he'd been poached to this firm on a huge salary.

Unfortunately, he had all the complexities of leadership in today's complex environment to deal with. He wasn't delivering what was most important. Everyone wanted a piece of him. He was ineffective at his priorities. He wasn't a melodramatic, whirling dervish like some busy people. He'd just got smothered by all the demands for his time.

Switch-tasking – the enemy in our midst

A study by the National Bureau of Economic Research in the US measured the working habits of 1,114 CEOs across six countries. On average, they spent just 5.3 minutes on each of their tasks, before they moved to the next. Wham, bam – a production line, with no deep thinking, just endless doing.

This is how Joachim spent his days, strangled by endless emails, messages and distractions from his global team and multiple stakeholders. I watched him work: he was a slave to technology. It was controlling him, not the other way round.

He had two screens, two iPhones and an iPad on his desk. He'd respond to a Teams message, then another, then go back to his designs, see a notification about an email and reply to it, then another couple, then he'd check the internet, go back to the design, respond to a WhatsApp and get another Teams message.

We all play this game of Whac-a-Mole. I bet you have a phone next to you now and are alert to anything new popping up. We delude ourselves we are multitasking and being uber-productive. We are not, we are switch-tasking: switching from one usually low-value task to another and back again.

Switching costs valuable time when we mentally transition from one task to another, then switch back to the original task. Recent estimates in the *Journal of Experimental Psychology* suggest we can lose up to 40 per cent of our productivity through this relentless game of Whac-a-Mole. Our brains can only concentrate on one cognitive task at once. Music may play while we work, but we can only focus fully on that work.

Technology saps our attention and has taken over our day, rather than being used as a helpful tool. Microsoft didn't invent Teams or Outlook for us to use them occasionally; the company wanted to make them essential. And we have become addicted to office technology, just as we are addicted to the apps on our phones. Our brains see messages and notifications as a threat, the modern woolly mammoth bearing down on us, so we respond to them to make them go away. The trouble is, the opposite is true: the more messages we send, the more we get back.

Energy company Ovo has reported that each UK adult sending one less 'thank you' email a day would save over 16,433 tonnes of carbon a year – the same as 81,1522 flights to Madrid or taking 3,3343 diesel cars off the road.

Dealing with this noise is how we know people are spending much longer at work than necessary – our tasks simply take longer.

Joachim had to get off the crazy busy bandwagon and carve out some quiet space for innovation, creativity and concentration. His teams needed it too.

Why it's so hard to think: the cognitive tax

Joachim admitted that even when he had time, he was finding it hard to concentrate, as if his brain had lost the habit of focusing. The more low-value tasks we do, the more we lower our capacity to deal with anything more challenging. We are paying a cognitive tax because of digitisation and the way we work.

I find this frightening. Joachim, like you and me, is a 21st-century 'knowledge worker', paid for the quality of his thinking but finding it hard to think because of the eco-system in which he works.

It's a truly vicious circle. We get so bogged down in low-value tasks that our brains can no longer handle the more significant ones.

We neglect strategic and problem-solving tasks, which cause us to be even busier down the line. A vortex of unproductivity with no quiet space in the middle.

We didn't need to work on Joachim's mindset. He was well aware of the consequences of continuing in this downward spiral. His professional reputation was at risk if he failed to rise above the demands on his time and create some space for concentrated, priority, creative tasks. He needed to create time for *flow*.

Fight the machine and get into flow

Researchers have a word for the state of deep hyper-focus when we are engrossed in our work: *flow*. Most of us have experienced a flow state through getting lost in a brilliant book, or studying for exams, or by swimming or running. We feel our best and perform our best, and it feels great. This used to be called *concentrating* and it wasn't such a big deal.

I wrote a long chapter on flow in *The Crazy Busy Cure*, explaining how hyper-concentrating like this releases the pleasure chemicals – dopamine, serotonin, endorphins, oxytocin, norepinephrine and anandamide. An abundance of free legal highs all at once, purely from doing our job. No need for free pizzas to make people happy: just allow them some peace to get on with their work.

Flow expert Stephen Kotler cites a ten-year study when executives reported they were five times more productive when they consistently worked in a flow state for one day a week. That's a huge expectation. The same researchers said that if we could all increase the time spent in flow by 15 to 20 per cent, overall workplace productivity would almost double.

Yet flow working isn't happening, mostly because we need to have a decent chunk of time when we aren't in a meeting. People tell me the best time of their week for deep work is a Sunday. It's absurd that we should have to use our own time for our most important work.

Another client once told me they had to fake a sick day to write a report. Their dinosaur director wanted them to be constantly available during work hours, so they felt they had no other way of getting some privacy.

Creating time for flow

Some functions are better than others at this. Sales and business development teams are more comfortable at locking themselves away for a couple of days to sprint through preparing pitches. These tasks are directly linked to making money, so maybe people find it more acceptable to be selfish and off grid.

One company I know has a system called 'jury service' that allows people to take time away from their day jobs to work wholeheartedly on another priority. The theory is that, as we are required to hand over work to colleagues when we are summoned to attend a court case for a couple of weeks, we can apply the same approach to fixing critical problems. It means doing the work once and doing it well because you have created space for it.

Joachim needed to find flow time with his team. I facilitated a *Crazy Busy* team session to figure out how they could pull this off.

We started with some magic questions.

'If you took yourselves more seriously as creatives, what would you do differently?'

'What difference would it make if you could have more time in flow?'

Once people saw the burning need for uninterrupted flow time, they had no problem in making space for it – and putting guard rails in place.

Time Management 101: schedule it, or it won't happen

This is how Joachim's team made time for flow in their complex international structure so they could all work effectively.

- They discussed their reliance on instant messaging and the culture they had created of constantly interrupting each other. They agreed to have more frequent catch-up calls and daily stand-up team meetings and to check their Trello project management boards for updates, rather than just firing off messages.

- They questioned the need to do everything synchronously. Decisions, brainstorms and celebrations should be in real time, but otherwise team members should have the flexibility to choose what task they did and when and where they did it, without interruption.

- They blocked out collective flow time, several times a week, when they would work on creative tasks – virtually or together in the office.

- The cleverest thing they did was rather than blocking their flow time out as *not available*, they highlighted other times in the calendar as *available*.

- They also agreed to do longer 'sprints' to work on creative projects, rather than trying to fit them in around routine schedules.

- If they were in the office, they would try to have lunch together, rather than remain at their screens. Problems get nipped in the bud more quickly over a sandwich than via a message thread.

- Joachim aimed to batch up his calls and do them all on a walk, encouraging his team to do the same. In 1889, philosopher Friedrich Nietzsche wrote: 'All truly great thoughts are conceived by walking.' Participants in a Stanford University study showed that walking allows the brain to wander, and 'opens up the free flow of ideas', an 81 per cent increase in divergent thinking.

To get into flow, many clients in smaller organisations simply decide the times of the week when they can have a couple of hours to themselves and then stick to it religiously. They switch off their apps and tell people when they will be back online. They know people will call if they are truly in need. Some monitored texts too. They might have a couple of interruptions, telling callers they'll ring back in an hour, then they quickly get back into flow. They get nothing but respect for this.

Leadership is a spectator sport, especially where carving time for flow is concerned. If your teams observe you creating time for doing high-quality work and deeper thinking, they will do the same. What difference would that make to your organisation?

Joachim and his team became far happier once they felt in control of their time and able to do what they did best.

Work less, plan more

When I ask people how much time they spend planning, it's a lot less than they'd like.

Taking time to reflect during the working day has been proven to increase productivity. Harvard Business School researchers found that when people added 15 minutes of reflection into the end of their working day – rather than working for those 15 minutes – their productivity increased by nearly a quarter in only ten days. That spike remained when reassessed a month later. The researchers concluded that getting more done was less effective than reflecting on the work people had already done.

Put your phone away and pause. Instead of reacting to everything around you, get back to the big questions.

'Why am I doing this?'
'Where do I add the most value?'
'What difference can I really make?'
'What's working well and what can I improve?'

Here are some useful questions to help someone add more value and find flow:

'What's your highest and best use?'
'If you took yourself more seriously, what would you do differently?'
'What difference would it make if you could spend more time in flow?'

Resources

Bandiera, O., Hansen, S., Prat, A. and Sadun R. (2017) National Bureau of Economic Research, *CEO Behaviour and Firm Performance,* working paper 23248, (March 2017, revised September 2017).

Everett, Z. (2022) *The Crazy Busy Cure*, Nicholas Brealey Publishing.

Oppezzo, M. and Schwartz, D.L. (2014) Give your ideas some legs: the positive effect of walking on creative thinking. *Journal of Experimental Psychology: Learning, Memory, and Cognition* 40(4): 1142–52. See: https://www.apa.org/pubs/journals/releases/xlm-a0036577.pdf (accessed 8 July 2024).

Kotler, S. and Wheal, J. (2018) *Stealing Fire,* Harper Collins.

Swainson, R., Prosser, L.J. and Yamaguchi, M. (2024) Preparing a task is sufficient to generate a subsequent task-switch cost affecting task performance, *Journal of Experimental Psychology: Learning, Memory, and Cognition* 50(1): 39–51.

Ovo Energy (online) Think Before You Thank report See: https://company.ovo.com/think-before-you-thank-if-every-brit-sent-one-less-thank-you-email-a-day-we-would-save-16433-tonnes-of-carbon-a-year-the-same-as-81152-flights-to-madrid/ (accessed 8 July 2024).

Chapter 11

———

Public speaking makes me anxious

- -

'Dear Zena

I get super anxious before social events. I worry for hours before them, and then afterwards I worry I said the wrong thing. I especially hate speaking in front of my board of directors, as I don't want to make a fool of myself. When I force myself to do it, I feel utterly self-conscious. I'm sure they can see me shake. I have a big budget meeting coming up and I'm dreading it. I can't duck out of it but can't bear them judging me.'

- -

Themes

- Social anxiety disorder
- Cognitive distortions
- Public speaking
- Perfectionism
- Confidence

Here's a case of behaviour that is 'bad' only in the sense that it hurts the person doing it. It's not hurting anyone else directly; it's mainly stopping one person from making their full contribution and diminishing their career.

Social anxiety disorder is a fear of social situations. It's more than just shyness and can become crippling. My client was doing first-class work at a senior level, but her anxiety was causing her noticeable distress.

Louisa was the UK finance director of a large international organisation. She was first class at her job but had a bumper mental block about speaking in public. She was fine in team meetings, but felt intimidated when presenting to very senior people. If possible, she would enlist someone to speak on her behalf. As she needed to present her budget at least twice a year, as well as speaking at other leadership meetings, her avoidance problem was snowballing.

Cognitive reframing

We explored what Louisa's inner voice was telling her. Her protective chimp brain – as consultant psychiatrist Professor Steve Peters calls it in *The Chimp Paradox* – was trying to save her from danger: *don't make a fool of yourself . . . they are going to shout you down . . . it's going to be horrible . . . don't do it!*

Perhaps your chimp is being rational, helping you to avoid danger. Listen to it. *You might need more preparation . . . don't wing it.* The answers are simple: practise, record your own voice and get feedback, go through some presentation skills training or voice coaching. Learn the skills.

Sometimes, it's straightforward over-thinking – all or nothing. We put way too much pressure on ourselves. Louisa admitted she wanted to knock each presentation out of the park, to give an amazing presentation that blew everyone's minds.

This was commendable, but excessive. No one had said anything about expecting the eloquence of Barack or Michelle Obama. After all, Louisa's brief was to talk through the main points of her budget, not over-complicate it, not bore people with too many slides and keep to time.

The perils of perfectionism

Perfectionists like Louisa aren't trying to be perfect. They just think that nothing they do is ever enough, that what they offer isn't worthy of the people they are offering it to.

Perhaps that's a helpful driver in areas like music, sport or art, but most of us just need to get our work done to a reasonable standard and pass it on to the person waiting for it. There are no prizes for perfection and no point in wasting precious time, trying to make things perfect that don't need to be. Save your energy for a hobby outside work if you need an outlet for being picky.

Public speaking pops up a lot in coaching as a career blocker. It's a skill that only improves with practise, so we need to encourage people to give presentations often and early in their careers. Make it low-stakes and relaxed and give people constructive feedback about whether they got their points across briefly and in a clear way. Anything more than that is a bonus. At some point, they might get to TED Talk standard, or be hilarious – although that may not be the best outcome for a budget delivery. Most of the time, people getting their message across is exceptional enough – and more than most people manage.

Louisa was demanding a perfect performance of herself. As a child, she was a medal-winning ice skater and the high standards that came with performing had stuck with her. Perfect 10s were her validation. As author and executive coach Marshall Goldsmith says in his seminal book, *What Got You Here Won't Get You There*, the high standards you set yourself early in life hold you back later. You are too busy now to make things perfect, especially if they aren't worthy of it.

Turning down opportunities to speak was Louisa's way of avoiding the shame of a less than perfect performance. Of course, it was sabotaging her career prospects by reducing her profile and puzzling her CEO, who expected more visibility from her finance director.

When we feel anxious like this, we make sweeping negative judgements, instead of looking rationally at where we can improve. Instead of dissecting what we did – *great opening question . . . they seemed engaged . . . next time I'll have a punchier call to action at the end* – we tell ourselves it was all rubbish, scoring a big F for failure.

Curiously, people who loathe speaking in public rarely practise enough when forced to do it. The excuse of not having enough time to prepare gives them a psychological get-out for a less-than-perfect performance.

Louisa could see that although she practised her ice-skating for hours as a child, she expected herself to be a polished speaker without minimal practise. She never did a dry run or rehearsal. It's the same reason procrastination is a red flag of perfectionism. They rush everything as a deadline looms, giving themselves a good excuse for a lacklustre result. If they'd taken their time, they'd have to cope with the discomfort of a task not panning out 100% the way they wanted.

I asked Louisa if she judged other people's presentations the way she was expecting them to judge her. Of course not. She turned up rooting for people to do well, not looking to criticise. She didn't pay close attention to the people. She listened to what they were saying and how that would impact her.

I reminded Louisa about my *Mind Flip* philosophy for career success. Work becomes easier and more meaningful when we stop thinking about our own issues and focus instead on the problems we can solve for others.

Could she think about her audience and how they would benefit from the information she gave them, rather than worry about herself? Her presentation wasn't about her. Renowned voice teacher and communication expert Caroline Goyder believes we should approach giving speeches as a service.

Louise could now look at her presentations with more objectivity. We did some practical work on defining the points she wanted to make and how she could get them across.

Confidence and acting *'as if'*

Confidence is a rear-view idea: we become confident only *after* we do things. If we wait until we are confident, we'd never try anything for the first time. Louisa needed to behave *as if* she was confident, even if she didn't feel it. I asked her what she would do if she were a confident speaker.

She wouldn't apologise when she spoke, she'd have a confident opening line to grab everyone's attention, she'd look sharp, she'd likely adopt a power pose, she'd speak clearly, rehearse professionally, ask for constructive advice and feedback, turn up early, make confident small talk before giving her talk, and so on. She had an impressive list.

I'm cautious about asking people what they'd have to lose by doing something. That can take them down a rabbit hole of catastrophes: they'd lose their professional credibility, their already fragile self-esteem, probably lose their job, their partner would leave them and take the kids and dog away forever . . . Good luck in getting someone out of that chasm.

I don't reassure clients that everything will always go swimmingly either. That's highly unlikely; in real life, things go wrong.

Theresa May, then UK Prime Minister, developed a hacking cough that wouldn't go away slap bang in the middle of what was supposed to be a rousing speech to her fellow Conservative MPs at the party's annual conference. And it got worse.

A prankster jumped onto the stage to protest by handing her a redundancy notice. At one point, her Chancellor of the Exchequer handed her a cough sweet. And she drew applause for croaking out that the only person she wanted to make redundant was her opposite number, Labour party leader Jeremy Corbyn.

But then the letters from the party slogan on the wall behind her fell off; it was a speech beyond rescue, one people will remember for the wrong reasons.

If we have strategies for things not going to plan, it makes us feel more confident. And if they go perfectly? Even better. Here's what I took Louisa through.

What's your greatest fear?

'I'm afraid I'll forget my words, start to cough and find I can't stop. The slides won't work, my neck goes bright red, and I break into a sweat.'

If that happened, what would you do?

'I'd have prompt cards, back up the slide deck, have water and cough sweets to hand, take a deep breath, and smile.'

How can you mitigate against disaster happening?

'I will drink only water before my talk, not coffee, to protect my voice. I'll allow more time to check everything, and have one of my team ready to step in if I really can't speak. And I'll wear a scarf and a lightweight jacket to cover up physical signs of stress.'

Social anxiety

I was interested in why there were certain audiences Louisa particularly dreaded presenting to. Most of us come across people who make us feel more uncomfortable, or less psychologically safe, than others. Perhaps there is something about those individuals or just because they are senior to us, and we feel they are in control of our entire destiny, even though they are most likely thinking about themselves and their stuff, not yours.

Dr Ellen Hendriksen is a clinical psychologist at Boston University's Center for Anxiety and Related Disorders and author of *How to Be Yourself.* She writes that social anxiety can convince us we have something wrong with us and that this 'fatal flaw' will be obvious to everyone else. They will judge and reject us for it.

Louisa acknowledged she was far more anxious about presenting to very senior men, who reminded her of judgemental authority figures earlier in her life. It didn't mean that she'd stop presenting to them, just that she would be aware they triggered her anxiety. Breathing techniques helped her to feel and sound in control.

Unhelpful beliefs

Louisa was worried that people would think her boring, realise her English – not her first language – wasn't good enough, and, of course, see that she was nervous. She had an entire list. We all have one. Whatever our perceived flaw, we are convinced it will be discovered, we'll be exposed and hauled over the coals for it.

Most of the time, our flaws are in our imagination, but we act is if they were true.

Louisa thought they were real, so she avoided the presentations she imagined would prove her to be right. Nancy Kline, author of *Time to Think,* which offers an amazing coaching process for challenging limited assumptions, deftly turns around these perceptions.

I asked Louisa if it was true that her English wasn't good enough. Of course, it wasn't. In that case, what was true?

What's true could only be the exact opposite: her English WAS good enough.

Looping back up to purpose

We ended Louisa's session by returning to her purpose and who would benefit from her giving presentations. Who would suffer consequences if she didn't?

If she didn't present her budget figures to the international big wigs, her UK subsidiary might not get the full allocation needed to make changes they wanted to implement. Her purpose was much bigger than avoiding making a speech, and that proved to be the clincher she needed to experience some discomfort.

Louisa delivered her presentation.

She asked for feedback from a couple of people she knew would have shrewd comments. She wasn't just looking for 'you were great' praise, but more helpful specifics that would help her hone her craft.

'What was the main takeaway you got from my session.'

'I think I could have skipped slide two; what else do you think I could change next time?'

In the same way that sports people reflect on how their victory felt so they can recreate the feelings the next time they compete, Louisa took five minutes to savour conquering her fears.

You may be rolling your eyes at this, but try it. We are great at remembering our mistakes, not so good at patting ourselves on the back and banking the victories.

Useful questions to boost confidence

This is the magic question.

'Imagine you were confident at giving presentations. How would you approach this one?'

Or one to ask to gain a more rational perspective.

'What's the worst that can happen? What would you do? How can you prevent that from happening?'

And if you want to flush out those paralysing fears . . .

'What do you think will be obvious to everyone else about you?'

Or to encourage people to talk about the background to their issue.

Could you tell me more about the situation, so I can understand it better?

Watch out for overstepping boundaries

Take care to be sensitive when exploring why people are stressed out by certain people or situations, as we did with Louisa's social anxieties. You are getting right to the heart of someone's insecurities and core beliefs.

- Don't ask unless invited. Have you been asked for help or feedback?

- Don't ask unless you feel competent to handle any emotion it brings up in them – or you.

- Don't dig for deeper answers that they don't seem ready to give you. They are under no obligation to share their thoughts with you.

- Don't dispute it, as in 'that's ridiculous, you're a total supernova'. They won't believe you anyway. Your job is to help that person come to the realisation that what they are saying isn't true and to find what's genuinely true instead. Correcting them won't make any difference. And you could make things worse by denying their feelings, just as they are being vulnerable and opening up.

- Don't ever bring it back to you, as in 'you think you've got problems, what about my big nose/geekiness/inadequacies.' This is not about you.

Read more about boundaries in Chapter 23.

Resources

Cuddy, A. (2016) *Presence,* Orion.

Everett, Z. (2020) *Mind Flip: Take the Fear out of Your Career,* Curlew House.

Goldsmith, M. (2007) *What Got You Here Won't Get You There,* Hyperion.

Goyder, C. (2020) *Find Your Voice: The Secret to Talking with Confidence in Any Situation,* Vermilion.

Hendricksen, E. (2019) *How to Be Yourself: Quiet your Inner Critic and Rise Above Social Anxiety,* St Martin's Griffin.

Kline, N. (2002) *Time to Think: Listening to Ignite the Human Mind,* Cassel.

Peters, S. (2012) *The Chimp Paradox,* Vermilion.

Stanhope, E. (2019) *Goodbye Glossophobia: Banish Your Fear of Public Speaking,* Filament Publishing.

Case studies: Colleagues behaving badly

Chapter 12

My manager is a two-faced frenemy

'**Dear Zena**

My manager pretends to be my best friend, but I've discovered she makes mean comments about me behind my back. Last week, she gave me cruel feedback out of nowhere, then sent me a gushing text message that night about how much she loved working with me. I love my job, but I don't trust her. How can I work with her?'

> # Themes
>
> - Boundaries
> - Frenemies
> - Office politics
> - Gossip

Annalise, in her early 30s, worked in a recruitment agency. Her office manager, Janice, in her 40s, was inconsistent towards Annalise, see-sawing between friendship and enmity. Jenna Abetz, a faculty member at the College of Charleston in South Carolina, has carried out research on frenemies. She defines them as unhealthy relationship patterns that appear friendly but are fraught with jealousy, competition and mistrust. This might be fun to watch in a fictional TV series; in the workplace, real people get hurt. The Annalise/Janice dynamic fitted the frenemy script to a tee.

At first, Janice lavished Annalise with overblown displays of attention and praise. They went out clubbing, Janice introduced Annalise to her friends and family, she sent her motivational quotes – *Pink isn't just a colour, it's an attitude!* – and posted pictures of them together with hashtags such as #dreamteam #champagne #success. Annaliese found it jarring, but was flattered by the older woman's attention.

On nights out together, Janice spent most of the time talking about herself, her troubled marriage and her other personal problems and fallings-out with people. After one weekend confessional, Janice sent Annalise a WhatsApp message saying that she always tried to be there for Annalise, but was upset at not being supported enough in return.

The mind-messing behaviour continued with hurtful 'teasing' disguised as compliments – 'that dress you've got on today actually looks quite good on you'. Barbed criticism came next, wrapped up as feedback, often followed by late-night messages about how they were *'soul-sisters'*, and maybe Annalise was *'too sensitive'*. Annalise felt as if she was back at school, navigating grisly teenage friendships.

Annalise bagged a couple of big clients. Although the entire office benefitted, Janice seemed less than overjoyed about Annalise's success. When Annalise stepped up to receive an award for her triumph at the company conference, Janice told others at their table that she'd carried out most of the work behind the scenes.

People shouldn't have to tolerate this crap. However, leaving the job would have meant Annalise letting down her new clients. She didn't want to miss out on her bonuses either. Janice's behaviour wasn't going to drive her away. She also knew it wasn't her job to manage Janice's moods: she had to manage her response to them.

We started our coaching by defining what Annalise wanted to accomplish in her career and what she was prepared to tolerate on the way to getting it. She felt back in control. During the next couple of months, Annalise worked on building healthy professional boundaries with Janice.

- Annalise's first step was to address the issue, not ignore it. She asked Janice to step out for coffee – not for lunch or for a chat after work, as she didn't want Janice to have a glass or two of wine and become ratty. She explained how Janice had hurt her feelings, that she wanted to remain working for her – knowing it would have been a disaster for Janice's career if top performer Annalise had moved on – but she'd prefer it if Janice gave her feedback in private. She said she knew Janice didn't intend to be hurtful, but that was the result of her behaviour. As expected, Janice denied she'd intended any harm, but Annalise had made her point.

- Then she won Janice over. Annalise told her how much she respected Janice's expertise and asked for help with some sales plans. Janice was flattered and probably relieved that she had something meaningful to contribute.

- Annalise kept Janice's messages and emails in case they were needed as evidence should the negative behaviour escalate. Annalise found reasons to email Janice's boss, always copying Janice in. Annalise took care to credit Janice, but made sure her own efforts were reaching the right people.

- She stopped responding to Janice's out-of-hours messages, unless they were genuinely important, which was almost never; if she replied she sent brief messages or just a thumbs-up. Annalise remained friendly and made small talk with Janice in the office, but avoided gossip and found reasons to be busy when she sensed Janice was keen to dump.

Annalise knew she was too good to become a player in Janice's games. When she took herself seriously and changed her behaviour, Janice changed her behaviour too.

Most people respond well when someone sets a boundary: *'I'm happy to share information with you, but I'm sure you understand I can't talk about other people's bonuses.'* This is discretion people appreciate.

If someone gets angry or tries to punish you for setting a boundary, it illustrates the unhealthy nature of the relationship. Stay firm on your limits, and don't capitulate. Accept that you might need a way of detaching from a negative relationship where only one person sets the boundaries, someone who isn't you. Boundaries are a crucial issue in relationships and I have a whole chapter dedicated to this (see Chapter 23).

Janice wasn't my client, so I can't say for sure what was going on in her head, but I suspect some of her behaviour came from vulnerability. She probably wasn't clear on how she ought to behave as a manager and developed needy relationships instead. Janice became more confident and professional when Annalise enlisted her help to plan valuable sales strategies. When Janice slipped back to making mean comments, Annalise, with her eyes firmly on bigger prizes, could rise above them.

There are simple ways to avoid taking unpleasant comments personally.

- Accept that when people say nasty things, it's about them, not you. They are projecting their feelings as a defence mechanism, accusing you of something they dislike in themselves.

- When someone's self-esteem is threatened, making them feel vulnerable, that person tries to fit into a group by creating situations where they can exclude others. Putting others down is a misguided way of feeling better about ourselves. Sarah Weart, who did a PhD on gossip at Yale University, found that when pairs of friends felt this kind of exclusion, they gossiped more harshly about a third person. This can escalate when that third person, or an entire group, retaliates or withdraws.

- People who feel good about themselves don't feel a need to criticise others. They've nothing to project. As author, founder of Peaceful Mind Peaceful Life, and social media celebrity Barb Schmidt puts it, hurt people hurt people.

- Accept that the more successful and visible you become, the more criticism you will attract. You will spark other people's envy. The more you share about yourself, especially on social media, the more ammunition you give others.

- If – and only if – you think someone's comments are worth attention, reflect on what they said. Ignore the intentions behind their comments, just consider if there's a grain of truth in their words. If there is, learn. If not, move on.

- Nurture your inner circle: relationships with people who have your back.

Resources

Abetz, J.S. (2023) Defining and exploring frenemy relationships, *Southern Communication Journal* 88(2).

Mills, C.B., Yu, P. and Mongeau, P.A. (2023) Frenemies: Acting like friends but feeling like enemies. *Western Journal of Communication* 1–21.

Weart, S. (2004) *Negative Gossip as a Response to Threatened Social Self-Esteem*, PhD dissertation, Department of Psychology, Yale University.

For more about handling mean comments and how hurt people hurt people, follow Barb Schmidt @peaceful_barb and her *Barb Knows Best* podcast.

Chapter 13

I work for a toxic narcissist

'Dear Zena

I don't know what I've done to annoy my CEO. We used to have a great relationship, but I'm feeling she's gone right off me. Her moods are impossible to predict. Sometimes she can be super nice, then out of the blue she'll be cold and uncommunicative. She has belittled me in front of my team, accusing *me* of poor communication. Then she'll be nice again. It's stressing me out. Is it me, or is it her? Am I being paranoid? This has never happened to me before.'

Themes

- Narcissistic personality disorder
- Co-dependency
- Bad bosses
- Bullying
- Scrappy careers
- Interoception

Commercial director Dan was headhunted to join the board of a prestigious non-governmental organisation. The charismatic new CEO, Tina, wooed Dan on the basis of her ambitious vision for the future, which Dan shared, and the vital part he could play in it.

Tina's impressive LinkedIn profile showed her glittering Oxbridge education and her previous high-ranking roles in the UK's Foreign Office. She was impressive in person: charming; attractive; and an accomplished presenter. The media loved her, and the numbers of her social media followers were through the roof. Everyone could see she was a perfect ambassador for the organisation and its charitable aims.

When Dan bagged the job, he could barely believe his luck. This was a strategic career move for him. His aim was to be CEO of a charity himself one day, and this was an excellent stepping stone. He hoped that some of Tina's gloss would rub off on him too; everyone seemed to idolise her. Sadly, if someone looks too good to be true, then they doubtless are.

Dan negotiated some coaching as part of his package to help him start with vigour. I was delighted to get the job.

Dan was smart, ambitious, excellent both at clarifying priorities and culling conflicting distractions. It was music to my ears. He rapidly earned the respect of his team and peers. He was confident, yet humble and self-aware.

The only fly in the ointment was that Dan was having trouble pinning down Tina to a meeting to agree to objectives.

Entrepreneur, TED Talk speaker and author of multiple books on leadership Margaret Heffernan says the entire construct of management is 'forecast, plan, execute'. This was second nature to Dan, but he needed to get his plan signed off by Tina so that he could get on with the execution phase.

It is hard to know what to deliver when you don't know your deliverables. It made Dan uneasy that he wasn't clear how Tina was measuring his performance. How was he to know if he was doing a good job in her eyes?

Dan was smart and experienced, so he put together his own plan and got on with it. It's not uncommon for CEOs like Tina to be so busy with external relations that they have little time for their senior team. Dan cut her some slack; she was newish in her role too. She seemed happy with him though, writing a glowing press-release about his appointment and arranging for meetings where he could meet the organisation's prestigious funders.

While Dan was getting his feet under the table, a couple of his co-directors left the organisation. Tina's harsh criticism of them surprised Dan at the first board meeting after they'd left; she slagged them off as useless, way past their best and she didn't want to waste resources on a leaving event for them.

None of this seemed compatible with the organisation's values – respect, integrity, kindness, etc. – and an awkward atmosphere filled the room. No one challenged Tina. In hindsight, that was a huge red flag: beneath Tina's pleasant patina lay a different person.

Dan and I worked together for six months. A year later, he got in touch again. I was stunned by the man I met. He seemed fragile, reduced somehow. He said he was more stressed about work than he'd ever felt in his career, even when he'd managed bigger teams and budgets.

Now, I enjoy dealing with data, but gut feeling is important too. I encourage my clients to tune into what their body is telling them. This perception of sensations from inside the body is called interoception. Messages from inside aren't as familiar as our external senses – sight, hearing, taste, touch and smell – but interoception is a growing area of interest for neuroscientists and psychologists.

Tension in our muscles, stomach clenching, our heartbeat, or a sixth sense that something isn't right when you walk into a room: this is all interoception. Your body is giving you subconscious messages before your brain has processed them. Dan had a physiological reaction to dealing with Tina before his brain figured out the problem. In Dan's case, it was a strong and unpleasant gut reaction, his intuition telling him that something was wrong. This wasn't a storm in a teacup; something much bigger was brewing.

Dan sensed Tina had a problem with him, although she hadn't given him that feedback. He felt that everything he did wasn't good enough for her. He still hadn't had the slightest clue about what she wanted from him, so he was 'shooting rabbits in the dark', as he put it.

Tina had declared how much she hated 'bad' news, so he and his co-directors learned to put a positive spin in their reports rather than invite a public dressing down, which had happened to one of his colleagues. This worried Dan; he'd never worked in an environment where he couldn't be open about problems, and he knew he had a responsibility to point out risks.

During the next few months, Tina hired replacements for the board members who'd left. She never missed an opportunity to sing their praises, just as she had with Dan at the start. At the same time, Dan's relationship with Tina soured.

Her mood was unpredictable, and he never knew how she'd respond to him. Sometimes she was charming, sometimes she'd ignore him.

Tina left Dan off the invitation list to a couple of meetings with her and her finance director; he felt he was being pushed out of her inner circle. Any lack of information would make it harder for him to perform well. His worries were now becoming a reality. Without having the full picture, Dan's performance was certain to slide.

The level of stress didn't help. Some cortisol enhances performance, but too much of it stifles our cognitive ability and other stress symptoms show up. We simply don't work well if we are stressed. Dan was sleeping poorly and said he felt on a continual short trigger with his family.

Although Tina was fine with Dan in their rare one-to-ones, she devalued his work before others, rolling her eyes and making sarcastic put-downs like, 'Dan is being his normal pernickety self' when he asked for detail or clarification.

I asked if he might be unnecessarily bogged down in the weeds? He said maybe, although he thought he was simply doing his job. I explained I was looking at the other side of the story, if there was one – not aiming to gaslight Dan by failing to take him seriously. That would make things even worse.

Dan complained to his wife about his relationship with Tina. She told him to stand up for himself. Dan asked to meet Tina and said he would prefer her to give him feedback in private. He also asked how they could work together more constructively. Sounds reasonable to me, but Tina denied the existence of any problem and brought the conversation to an abrupt halt.

Confronting Tina was the worst thing Dan could have done.

The gloves were off.

At the next meeting, she talked over Dan and bluntly rejected a proposal he'd made, contradicting a previous agreement to give him the budget for it.

The give-away: treading on eggshells

Dan felt humiliated. It was as if he'd woken a dormant snake. Then he said the magic words that proved he was in a relationship that went beyond 'ordinary' bullying: he felt he was *treading on eggshells* around Tina.

We know how to deal with playground bullies. You stand up for yourself. Dan was now experiencing far nastier abuse, with different rules. Tina was unpredictable and inconsistent: sometimes she was nice, sometimes plain nasty. All this does is stir up self-doubt and anxiety. Dan was the frog, being boiled slowly in a pot of horrible toxic abuse.

I am not qualified to give a diagnosis, especially about someone I haven't met, but this seemed like classic narcissistic behaviour.

Narcissistic Personality Disorder – when it's the real thing

People often bandy around the narcissist tag in pop culture to describe politicians and ex-partners we've decided are deplorable. As clinical psychologist Dr Monica Johnson says in her *Savvy Psychologist* podcast, those people are probably jerks, not fully fledged narcissists.

Narcissistic Personality Disorder (NPD) is a personality disorder thought to occur in less than 2 per cent of the general population. NPD is more common in males than females, but that doesn't mean there aren't female narcissists, just fewer of them. High-functioning narcissists are often ambitious and successful, so it's not uncommon to find them in senior leadership or entrepreneurial roles at the top of the tree. I've met several in my career.

NPD is characterised by extreme grandiosity and self-importance, an excessive need for admiration, an unrealistic sense of capability and value and a pronounced lack of empathy. Many of us have developed some narcissistic tendencies to survive corporate life.

Having these characteristics does not qualify you as someone with NPD. An embellished LinkedIn profile is common practice, but it doesn't put you in this category of having NPD.

Working for someone with this disorder puts you in an intensely unpleasant, emotionally abusive relationship that risks damaging your mental health. If you are unlucky enough to have been through this kind of relationship, you will already know what I mean. You feel like the rug is being pulled from under your feet, but you don't know why. You often ask yourself: 'Is this me?'

I've noticed common patterns when I've coached clients with similar stories to Dan.

Ask yourself if the following has ever happened to you.

- You were hired by a charming, accomplished person like Tina, perhaps at the top of the organisation as the founding entrepreneur.

- At the start, they made you feel special. But over time, you sensed they weren't satisfied with your work, although you couldn't improve because their expectations were vague.

- Sometimes you knew your ideas were on the right track, but only because your boss took credit for them. If you pointed this out, they turned on you, accusing you of being over-sensitive. If you have ever googled 'am I over-sensitive' it's unlikely you are the problem.

- They fuss over the newest member of the team and simultaneously devalue the work you do, perhaps in public.

- They blame others for their mistakes. They have extreme feelings about other people too – they are flawless or written off as useless, even plain enemies. People are with them, or against them.

- They rewrite history, remember situations and conversations differently to how things happened. You question yourself, often thinking: 'Is this me, or . . . ?' This is gaslighting.

- They accuse *you* of behaviours you have observed in *them*. You are the harsh one, the poor communicator, the one who upsets people. US psychologist Dr Jennifer Freyd defined this manipulation as DARVO: 'Deny, Attack and Reverse Victim and Offender'. The abuser denies the abuse took place, then attacks the person for attempting to hold them accountable or accuses the person of behaviour they've laid at their door. At this point they reverse roles, claiming they are the victim and blaming you for abuse.

- They cold-shoulder you, cutting you out of projects and taking you off the list for meetings and emails. They push you out of the tent.

- If challenged, they deny all accusations and fiercely criticise your behaviour, even suggesting that you bully them. This is classic gaslighting behaviour.

- Everyone else appears to idolise him or her, regularly praising them. You fear you are going a little crazy.

- You take time off sick, which is unusual for you. The most common symptoms I hear about are muscular pains, migraines and digestive problems, but stress manifests in multiple ways.

- You find it hard to move on because you crave their validation. You hope that one day you'll get it and keep trying to please them.

- Over time, your shame increases as your self-esteem declines. You wonder what happened to the go-getting, ambitious, positive person you used to be.

Standing up to them, especially in public, makes them worse. The standard advice on dealing with bullies doesn't work with a narcissist. Challenging them escalates the abuse. They have no empathy, so they don't care how their behaviour makes you feel. All they care about is how good you make them look. Your misery makes them feel better.

The best thing you can do in any toxic relationship is to get out of it. If that's not workable, you must distance yourself as much as possible. Find a side project in the organisation that involves you working more closely with other people.

These kinds of toxic relationships can trigger our shame or imposter syndrome, which may be lurking barely beneath the surface at best. I worked with Dan to help him feel in control and to avoid taking the situation personally, while reassuring him that none of this was his fault.

Scrappy careers – hopping through safe ground

I see careers as a leap from one patch of safe ground to another, my scrappy careers theory. We must own each patch and make the most of it before we move on to the next. Dan's leap into this NGO had been useful in getting him experience in the non-profit sector and in building new networks. When the right time came, he would be poised to pivot.

Until this point, Dan's career had gone precisely to plan, but that's no guarantee it would continue unabated. Some kind of hiccup is to be expected on the way to success and Dan needed to be resilient. That demands flexibility rather than positivity. Dan also had validation that, apart from the problem with Tina, the job had been fruitful by every other measure.

I encouraged Dan to do some low-key detective work into Tina's relationships with other people. Was Dan the only person to get this treatment? How genuinely popular was she? She had brought none of her previous colleagues with her when she joined the organisation. Dan realised she didn't appear to have any close business relationships, merely people who hung round her, flattering her for their own ends. Strong characters didn't seem to hang around her for long. She wasn't singling him out and it was important he understood this.

Moving on – planning a way to survival

Tina wasn't going to change. Was he prepared to accept and tolerate his situation? Why would he?

We talked about co-dependency. Co-dependents are people who allow themselves to be controlled or manipulated by others. They are natural magnets for narcissists, who can't survive without people feeding their ego; co-dependents give up their own needs to fuel those demanded by the narcissist. It's a perfect match.

If you have a tendency to put others' needs before your own, always trying to fix things for them and wanting to please, then you are displaying co-dependent behaviour. This makes you the natural other half in a relationship with a narcissist. You may have had similar relationship patterns earlier in your life.

All of this resonated with Dan, but he already felt depleted and didn't want to stick around longer than necessary. He felt Tina's behaviour was escalating. By the time he found another role and handed in his notice, he'd have been there for more than two years.

I was overjoyed to hear this. I've met people in similar circumstances who have become isolated, stressed and anxious. Obviously, this harms their career, their mental health and their other relationships. Ideally, you'd flag the person's behaviour to higher-ups, but if they are a powerful figure in the organisation, which is usually the case, this is difficult and can backfire. I've seen it happen where a complainant was packed off on sick leave during an investigation. They weren't sick. They were stressed as a result of behaviour that amounted to emotional abuse. The sick leave made them feel worse. Classic DARVO – turning everything around and putting the blame on the victim.

When keeping up pretence is the right thing to do

Dan kept up the pretence with Tina. People like her rarely change; we need to change our response to them. Narcissists have a powerful vision of who they think they should be and their behaviour stems from their shame of not living up to this ideal.

Bursting a narcissist's bubble is the worst thing you can do. Their response to any challenge will be aggressive and vengeful, as we've seen. Don't let them know you've seen through the mask: they will do anything to save face. A desire for vengeance can lead to extreme emotions. Professor Andrew Silke is Chair in Criminology at Royal Holloway, University of London; his area of expertise is political violence in Northern Ireland. He wrote he had never seen a serious act of violence that wasn't provoked by the experience of feeling shamed or humiliated and didn't represent an attempt to prevent or undo a loss of face, no matter how severe the punishment would be.

Presumably, Dan wasn't at risk of being the target of violence or attempted murder. But he still had to manage his exit with dexterity, to avoid Tina losing face. He stroked her ego as much as he could, without appearing creepy, and never criticised her. He kept his head down and got on with his work.

Meanwhile, he contacted people he could trust in his network and snagged a job offer from an organisation he had worked for previously. He returned at the same level he'd had before. It was a lateral move, but not a retrograde one. Most importantly, he returned to safe ground, with straight-forward people he could happily report to while rebuilding his sanity and confidence.

Does it surprise you how one rotten apple can have so much impact?

Toxic behaviour will only get nastier

If you employ one of these toxic people, then understand their behaviour will likely get nastier. You won't be able to ignore it for long. Honest feedback about their behaviour will be hard to find because people fear repercussions. You will find clues, particularly in your employee retention numbers. Find a reason to move them out before they do more damage to your organisation's culture and reputation. If you can't afford to lose their positive aspects – like business development strengths – shift them back to an individual contributor role where they will enjoy being a Captain Fantastic for bringing in results without hurting other people.

Useful questions to figure out if it is you or if it is them

Has this ever happened to you before?
What's your gut telling you?
Is there another side to your story?
What do you suspect that you'll know for definite in a few months?

Resources

Barlow, D. (2021) *Gaslighting & Narcissistic Abuse Recovery: Recover from Emotional Abuse, Recognise Narcissists & Manipulators and Break Free Once and for All*, Self-published.

Cameron, O.G. (2002) *Visceral Sensory Neuroscience: Interoception*, Oxford University Press.

Freyd, J.J. and Birrell, P.J. (2013) *Blind to Betrayal: Why we fool ourselves we aren't being fooled*, Wiley.

Heffernan, M. (2020) *Unchartered: How Uncertainty Can Power Change*, Simon & Schuster UK Ltd.

Hill, L. (2022) *Recovery from Narcissistic Abuse, Gaslighting, Codependency and Complex PTSD* (4 books in 1), Independently published.

Johnson, M. (2024) *The Savvy Psychologist Podcast*. Episode 416: The facts of narcissistic personality disorder.

Kirschbaum, C., Pirke, K.M. and Hellhammer, D.H. (1993) The 'Trier Social Stress Test' – a tool for investigating psychobiological stress responses in a laboratory setting, *Neuropsychobiology* 28(1–2) 76–81. https://doi.org/10.1159/000119004

Robson, D. (2021) *The Intelligence Trap: Revolutionise Your Thinking and Make Wiser Decisions*, Hodder & Stoughton.

Silke, A. (2003) *Terrorists, Victims and Society: Psychological Perspectives on Terrorism and its Consequences*, Wiley.

Chapter 14

I'm the office scapegoat

- -

'Dear Zena

My new line manager blames me for everything that's going wrong and belittles me in front of my team. I'm bending myself out of shape, trying to figure out what he wants. I'm the scapegoat for everything that goes wrong. It's making my life a misery, wrecking my confidence and I am worried this will impact my career prospects. How can I get back in control?'

- -

Themes

- Bad bosses
- Lateral moves
- Confidence
- Office scapegoat

Most of the problems so far have been about helping the client reframe their grasp of what's going on. This reframing of our beliefs is the foundation of cognitive behavioural coaching and therapy. As Einstein said: 'What we perceive as real is a cognitive distortion based on how we see the world.' Every conflict – if there is one – has two sides. It's just not always clear who is the culprit.

In Chapter 5, Rohit thought his team was over-sensitive, even though the problem was how insensitive he was. Curtis might have assumed in Chapter 8 that Ellie was slacking, when the truth was she was doing way too much. Most of coaching is like this – challenging assumptions, getting to the facts, pointing out blind spots and distorted thinking. Basic detective work, but minus the blood and dead bodies.

In this dilemma, Rory's perception was spot on; his manager Denis really seemed to have it in for him.

Rory was a management accountant, with a small team reporting to him. Rory had had a great relationship with the previous finance director, but his successor, Denis, didn't share the same confidence. Quite the opposite. Within a month of Denis joining the organisation, Rory got more critical feedback than he'd ever had before. Denis ignored the big stuff that Rory did right. Instead, he nit-picked the small stuff, almost for the sake of it. He seemed to scrutinise Rory's output far more than he did for other managers who reported to him, even though Rory was more experienced.

Rory's hunch was that Denis planned to launch a performance management process against him, without justification. He had sent Rory a highly critical email and copied in his entire team. When Rory asked for a meeting to discuss the email, Denis refused. He wanted Rory to fix the problems, not question his authority.

The final straw for Rory was when someone was recruited from outside to manage a bigger team. Rory's previous director had told him he was the natural successor for that role when it came up. Denis hadn't bothered to make Rory aware of the recruitment process going on, and rolled his eyes when Rory questioned why he'd been sidestepped.

This was making Rory doubt himself. He'd never been in a bruising situation like this before. He had a young family, had sweated to give them a good life and he felt like his stable foundations were being shaken.

We didn't know what was going on. Naïve assumptions lay thick on the ground. Maybe Denis was threatened by Rory? Maybe he wanted Rory to leave so he could bring in one of his own people as a replacement? Maybe Denis was too close to Rory's predecessor? It was turning into *Game of Thrones*.

Rory didn't want to stick around for more of this treatment. He was sure he wasn't being over-sensitive, and others could see he was being blamed for everything and was becoming an easy scapegoat.

In theory, Rory could have asked HR for support, but he had little confidence in HR having the expertise to tackle Denis without it backfiring on him. He didn't want to go over Denis's head and complain to senior management.

Rory just wanted to get away fast before Denis gave him a negative performance review that would stick on his records. He wanted to get back in the driving seat. I was pleased to hear this; I've seen people struggling to make the best of similarly unpleasant situations. Sometimes they survive relatively intact because their manager finds another punchbag, but survival comes at some expense to someone's self-esteem. Why stick round and stagnate under a poor manager if you don't need to?

Rory showed his mettle. He had no intention of staying put and being sucked down. He started the moving-on process, what he called Operation GTFO – get out fast, or words to that effect.

The magic question again was to remind him he was a high achiever.

'If you knew your next career move would be a resounding success, what would your next step be?'

Rory wanted to stay in the organisation as it offered great global career prospects and, apart from one rotten apple, he'd only good things to say about the leadership team.

As HR seemed a weak option, Rory seized the initiative himself. He is a lovely guy, one fortunate in having great relationships within the organisation. He found a lateral opportunity within a newly acquired subsidiary. It reported to a different finance director, one with whom he'd already had earlier contact. This got him back on track, in a well-functioning team where his contribution was valued. He never looked back.

Useful questions to help regain control

- *What's behind the other person's behaviour?*
- *If you knew your next role would be a great success, what would you do?*
- *Where is it written in the universe that life will always be fair?*

Chapter 15

My manager is too soft and the way she works is chaotic

- -

'Dear Zena

My manager does too much, mostly at the last minute. She never stops working and messages me throughout the night and at weekends. She is always in a rush, and doesn't listen properly, so the entire team keeps dropping the ball because we don't get proper instructions. She is doing my head in. She gets on with her own work but doesn't seem to realise she's supposed to manage the entire team's output. How can someone so smart be so chaotic? I really like her, but I can't work out what's going on with her.'

- -

Themes

- Neurodiversity
- Feedback
- Difficult conversations

Sue was the chief information officer in a management consultancy. Ana had some direct reports of her own, and was a project manager reporting to Sue. Ana was incredibly organised, as you'd expect from a project manager. Sue was not.

Sue was in meetings all day, every day, with little or no time to do actual work. She took on too much, was easily distracted, worked all hours, rushed through everything, and never slowed down to think or plan. She simply didn't have enough time to communicate with her team.

Sue's chaotic way of working was overwhelming the entire department. They had too many competing projects and no time to take in what was going on across the business so they could align priorities. They could barely keep up with service requests.

Ana felt they should be looking ahead more, anticipating future business needs to maintain competitive advantage. She worried about her own development and reputation for failures in doing this. She knew Sue's peers were realising there was a problem. Sue seemed to be drowning. Her stellar qualifications and superb past performance were at odds with her current problematic behaviour.

I asked Ana what her gut was telling her about Sue. This is a good way to get logical, data-driven people like Ana to tap into another significant source of information: her instincts. She felt Sue was heading for a melt-down because she was spinning too many plates.

Ana had to fix how she could work with and around Sue to meet her professional responsibilities healthily. How could she raise these sensitive topics with a more senior person?

Feedback models you may want to use

You may have come across one structure for doing this already.

When you do (x), it makes me feel (y), therefore please can you (insert different behaviour)?

This works well with emotionally intelligent people who are sensitive to your needs. Those who are more resistant may roll their eyes because it sounds too much like therapy-speak. Chances are, they may switch off.

A client gave me a fabulous alternative opening line for any conversation where you are asking for behaviour change.

I've noticed . . .

You are discussing behaviour you want to change, rather than making it a personal criticism.

I've noticed you often message me at the last minute with information you need for a meeting. How about we have a quick catch-up twice each week so I know what you need in advance and can plan around you? That's less stressful for me and generates better-quality information for you.

Ana had a sensitive, constructive conversation with Sue and used the *'I've noticed . . . '* opener to raise the topic. Sue was up for it and seemed pleased to discuss the practicalities of workflow management. She agreed she needed to communicate better with Ana and the rest of the team, too.

They agreed to have a quick coffee to catch up on Tuesday mornings when they were in the office together, plus a call every Friday. Yes, it's amazing this wasn't already in place, but I've never worked in any organisation that felt they had meeting frequency exactly right. Someone always raises poor comms or managers not spending solid, constructive time with their teams.

My feelings are more frequent meetings and catch-ups are often essential to spot and solve problems early and make sensible decisions, but it's important to make these meetings energetic. One of the best managers I've worked with makes a point of eating lunch with her team when they are in the office together. They chat and get to know each other and solve work issues effortlessly, when other people waste time sending emails that generate a time-wasting thread.

At our next coaching session – we worked at roughly three-weekly intervals – she said Sue had missed a couple of Friday calls but had blocked out time for future weeks and acknowledged the benefit of them.

During the same conversation, Ana tactfully explained to Sue that her constant emailing and messaging was distracting. Unbelievably, for someone with her information-based job role, Sue admitted to being inept with Outlook; she was too impatient to discover the useful nuances of the software. Ana showed her how to schedule her emails being sent at a reasonable business hour, instead of sending them immediately, no matter the hour.

She also suggested that Sue checked more often on the project management tools used by the team; she could get information herself, instead of interrupting others for progress reports. I often hear of senior people who aren't confident users of their systems. It slows their own work and everyone else's. This was the case with Sue, who said she didn't have the patience to attend the all-hands training. This might have been a waste of her time anyway as she probably didn't need to use all the software functionality, but no training had been scheduled to show team leaders how to use the system for management information.

This issue crops up repeatedly in my coaching sessions. Organisations spend fortunes on new systems, then cut the training budget that would allow people to make the most use of these tools. Ana organised a virtual session for all senior leaders to show them how to use the tools to increase productivity.

Understanding neurodivergence in the workplace

Remember that I wasn't coaching Sue, and we don't know what she was thinking or how she was feeling. My job was supporting Ana in how she responded to Sue.

Ana was now doing a good job in managing upwards. She had respect for Sue, despite the differences in how they worked. Although Sue was infuriating to work with because she appeared chaotic and didn't seem to listen properly, she had an exceptional ability to pinpoint solutions to complex issues. Her brain appeared to work on an original track.

Everyone has their own way of thinking, but most of us are considered neurotypical, to a greater or lesser degree. Others who often have some exceptional abilities are considered neurodivergent. This often presents through common conditions including dyslexia, dyspraxia, autism, OCD, ADHD and Tourette's syndrome.

These conditions present themselves in different ways, perhaps in our ways of learning, communicating, concentrating, risk-taking, impulsiveness, social preferences and how we perceive our environment. If you investigate the relevant signs, you may recognise many of them in yourself; it doesn't mean you are neurodivergent.

Many of these conditions are misdiagnosed or not diagnosed at all. A doctor's appointment is usually the first place to start if you feel it would be helpful. I am not a specialist in neurodivergence, nor can I diagnose any of these conditions, especially not for Sue, who I hadn't even met. And I don't like labels. However, there were enough flags here to imagine that looking into these different working styles was important.

At our third session, I asked Ana more about Sue's way of working. Ana was experienced enough to have wondered if Sue had an element of neurodivergence, although she was clearly highly functioning. She was a smart senior person; she wasn't disorganised because she couldn't be bothered. There had to be something else going on.

Neurodivergent brains are wired differently. In my experience, they are wired better than most. Many of the talented people I meet tell me they have some neurodiversity: that's often why they are hired, for their exceptional analysis and brainpower. What they need is empathy and some easy workarounds; what they don't need is being made to feel ashamed that they aren't 'normal' because they process, concentrate or communicate differently.

Most people-driven departments realise this and make efforts to support neurodivergence, make reasonable adjustments and even hire for it. Some are enlightened enough to celebrate it. They grasp the hard commercial facts about neurodiversity. Exceptional thinkers make all the difference to performance and profitability.

Ana clearly couldn't steam into Sue with an amateur diagnosis of how her brain worked; it would have been rude, unkind and presumptuous. She asked Sue a straightforward question that we should all ask each other.

How could we work better together?

This is a tactful, practical way of starting conversations about email use, changing meeting or one-to-one cadence, missed deadlines and poor communication: it's a way of covering anything that feels awkward to bring up.

They discussed how Sue could be more involved in the exciting idea-generating part of projects, and skip those meetings focused on mundane project management. This freed up space in Sue's calendar to plan and think – it was her superpower. Leadership and emotional intelligence coach Alina Addison, mother to a son on the autism spectrum, nails this in her book *The Audacity Spectrum*, highlighting proven methods that help to identify things that set us apart and inspire others.

Ana felt Sue was relieved they'd had this discussion.

The most important outcome of our coaching was that Ana was far less frustrated with Sue. She now had more respect for her. Ana was much more tolerant and happy to create workarounds that allowed Sue to use her problem-solving skills to the benefit of the entire team.

I was proud of Ana's maturity in how she handled this. She is well on the way to a stellar leadership career. She already had a supportive mentoring relationship with another senior leader in the business and she has used the relationship to fill gaps where Sue might not have useful insights.

Try these reflexive questions to figure out interpersonal challenges

- What is your instinct/gut telling you about this situation?
- What are the consequences of continuing like this, and avoiding dealing with it?
- What do you think is behind the other person's behaviour?

Useful ways to start a conversation about conflicting working styles

- How can we work better together?
- How do you like to work?
- What do you need from me?

Resources

Addison, A. (2024) *The Audacity Spectrum: Leading with Care, Courage and Non-Conformity,* Profile Books.

Everett, Z. (2021) Chapter 16: Invisible productivity problems, *The Crazy Busy Cure,* Nicholas Brealey.

Honeybourne, V. (Illustrated, 2019) *The Neurodiverse Workplace: An Employer's Guide to Managing and Working with Neurodivergent Employees, Clients and Customers*, Jessica Kingsley Publishers.

Young, S. and Bramham, J. (2012) *Cognitive-Behavioural Therapy for ADHD in Adolescents and Adults: A Psychological Guide to Practice,* Wiley-Blackwell.

Chapter 16

I'm not good enough for this role

'Dear Zena

I've been promoted, but I don't think I'm up for the job. There must have been other candidates with way more experience. I've no idea what they saw in me. It's only a matter of time before they realise I'm out of my depth. I'm so worried about not making mistakes, I'm procrastinating and doing very little.'

Themes

- Imposter syndrome
- Importance of clear job descriptions
- Dunning–Kruger effect
- Procrastination

Jake worked in procurement for a famous global drinks brand. His performance had been recognised with a substantial promotion. He contacted me because he felt he wasn't good enough for the job, a classic imposter syndrome feeling. This – if you didn't know – is when you doubt your abilities and feel you are going to be rumbled as a fraud. You feel you're the idiot in the room.

For most of us, it's a blip, a short-lived experience when we feel out of our depth in new situations or roles. It disproportionately affects high-achieving people, so take your visiting imposter as reassurance that you have joined this elite group. Professor Carter Cast, Clinical Professor of Entrepreneurship at the Kellogg School of Management, says poorer performers substantially overestimate their abilities, whereas strong performers underestimate theirs.

The positive side of imposter syndrome

I don't feel imposter syndrome is always a bad thing; it may even be helpful. I advised Jake to listen to what this feeling of uncertainty was telling him. Maybe it was his gut feeling, protecting him from failure. Did it have a point? Did he need to take a step back, get up to speed more quickly, or build a stronger team around him? What blind spots could he be missing?

And maybe that inner voice was wrong. Feelings aren't facts. Jake's bosses weren't fools. They knew what they were doing when they promoted him.

Jake felt a bit out of his depth, but that's healthy. We face new situations and challenges constantly. I asked Jake what he had done in similar new situations. It's helpful to remind people they can survive discomfort and repeat strategies that have worked for them previously.

I also asked if Jake was piling pressure on himself. He admitted he liked to know everything, wanted to be the smartest person in the room and have all the answers. We discussed if this was realistic or even desirable at this stage of his career.

Jake accepted the last thing his business needed was more over-confident know-it-alls. A much better option was to build trust in the abilities of his team; they had expert knowledge in specialised areas. He was fortunate to be surrounded by seasoned people. They didn't need Jake to tell them what to do. They wanted development and career opportunities. Jake was so good at his job, he'd already canvassed his team on what they really wanted, without relying on assumptions.

If you don't know what a good job looks like, how can you do one?

As often happens at senior level, Jake didn't have a new job description that accurately reflected his responsibilities. Neither did he have a clear reporting structure. How could he know if he was meeting expectations if he didn't know what they were? He needed a reliable yardstick by which he could measure if he was good enough – or not.

People are more likely to doubt their competence and contribution if they aren't clear on what people expect of them. The sensitive among us will always feel we haven't carried out a good job if we don't know how to measure what a good job is.

I see this often when clients have been in organisations for a long time and taken on other responsibilities; they've lost the idea of how they're being measured. Or they work in a complex matrix and can't figure out who has real influence, this being the person they should aim to satisfy. This is a reminder that you can't please everyone, so find out the key people where that's vital.

Jake wrote a job description and presented it to the person he was accountable to, along with half-yearly expectations that he could measure his performance against.

He asked him: *If I was the best hire you've ever made, what will I have achieved in a year's time?* A question that takes failure off-the-table is a great one to ask at interviews, too.

The interviewer will imagine how good you'll make *them* look in a year's time and will love all the problems you'll solve for them. They won't want to take the job away from you, even mentally. This used to be called a puppy-dog close, when the besotted client doesn't want to give the puppy back to the salesperson. I'm sure there's a more sophisticated name for it now, but think of those adorable retriever's eyes staring back at you.

Back to Jake. He could now stop worrying about over-compensating in areas where his team was doing a splendid job and put his energy

16 I'm not good enough for this role

into setting up a task force to identify the efficiencies artificial intelligence could bring to his procurement function. His focus shifted to thinking ahead, showing up as an outstanding performer.

I often meet talented mid-career professionals like Jake, who have confidence wobbles. They measure themselves against their peer group and feel they fall short.

Some of their less effective colleagues don't seem to be worried at all. They think they know it all. They are unencumbered with any doubt, the opposite of imposter syndrome.

Why stupid people think they know best

This is the confidence brought on by the Dunning–Kruger effect.

In 1995, two bank robbers in Pittsburgh called McArthur Wheeler and Clifton Earl Johnson tried to rob two banks. Their only disguise was to smear lemon juice on their faces, convinced that it would make them invisible to security cameras. Their approach and subsequent arrests intrigued social psychologists David Dunning and Justin Kruger, who studied the case to understand how people so hapless could be so confident.

They asked a group of students to complete self-evaluations in three areas: humour, grammar and logical reasoning. They compared the student assessments with their actual skills. The findings were clear: the most gifted students underestimated their abilities, while the least able overestimated theirs. This cognitive bias became the Dunning–Kruger effect: people with limited competence greatly overestimate their ability.

Don't be fooled by the foolish

I'm a huge advocate of the growth mindset: our abilities aren't fixed and can be developed with hard work. But the

Dunning–Kruger bias gives power to the wrong people. It's downright dangerous for unqualified self-help gurus to spout health advice, or for political leaders to make decisions with a limited grasp of their brief.

Have you seen people talk themselves into roles that are way beyond their current capability and fail to ask advice from the skilled people around them? Or a 'new broom' rocking a steady boat during the first months in a job because they think they know better? That's Dunning–Kruger in action. When you think you know it all, you aren't interested in the other side of the argument, the 'so-called expert' one.

> **'The whole problem with the world is that the fools and fanatics are so certain of themselves, and wiser people so full of doubts.'**
>
> **Bertrand Russell (1951)**

If you see Dunning–Kruger happening in your organisation, praise expertise and sponsor education. Create a genuine learning environment and encourage reflection. Empty vessels make a lot of noise: the vocal minority may be wrong. Get people like Jake to speak up in meetings and don't be swayed by soundbites when making decisions. Check your facts.

Try the following question to remind yourself that you can cope:

'Have you been in this situation before and what did you do?'

Or try these questions to encourage a switch from over-thinking to planning:

'If your role was a resounding success, what will you have achieved by this time next year?'

'If you were an outstanding performer in this role, where would you focus your attention?'

And don't forget this killer question to ask an interviewer:

'If I was the best hire you'll ever make, what will I have achieved in a year's time?'

Are you a genuine imposter?

There are times when if you feel like an imposter, you are one. Your feelings of not belonging may well be genuine.

If you don't have role models who are like you, or your competence is regularly and unfairly questioned, or you sense a bias against you, then of course you'll feel like an imposter. It's a vicious circle: once you feel like you don't belong, you act to fit that feeling. Marginalisation becomes a reality.

Inevitably imposter syndrome will be on the agenda when I am asked to speak at women's networking events. It rarely comes up in career strategy sessions in male-dominated workplaces.

That's not to say that men don't feel out of their depth as Jake did, but chances are that (white) men enjoy more validation over the years than many female counterparts, especially if male role models outnumber women at senior level.

One of my clients was told: 'You could be just as good as any of the guys here.' The comment may have been well-intentioned, but it was certainly ill-judged.

You know about this bias already. What can you do about it? How can you change your workplace culture?

Resources

Cast, C. (2018) *The Right and Wrong Stuff: How brilliant careers are made and unmade,* Public Affairs, Hachette Book Group.

Dweck, C. (2017) *Mindset: Changing the Way you think to Fulfil your Potential* (6th edition), Robinson.

Kruger, J. and Dunning, D. (1999) Unskilled and unaware of it: how difficulties in recognizing one's own incompetence lead to inflated self-assessments, *Journal of Personality and Social Psychology* 77(6): 1121–34.

Chapter 17

I'm covering for a
lazy colleague

- -

'Dear Zena

What do I do about my deadbeat colleague? All Dylan does is send Teams and Slack messages and stare at his phone. He's away from his desk a lot and I've never known anyone take so many bathroom breaks. I don't know how he gets away with it. I don't want to throw him under the bus, but it's not fair.'

- -

Themes

- Lazy co-worker
- Accidental manager
- Conflict avoidance
- Fear of negative valuation
- Difficult conversations

My client Remi and her frustrating colleague Dylan worked in the back office of a wholesale insurance broker. Remi was my client; I could only tackle the problem from her viewpoint. But that doesn't mean we couldn't dig into the reasons why people sometimes behave like Dylan.

Causes of lazy behaviour

Team members are usually aware of lazy colleagues before managers spot them because people like Dylan can appear super busy without doing much at all. Rarely does anyone set out intending to be deliberately lazy or doing a poor job. However, I'd love to get your opinion on this issue, and my contact details are in the front of the book.

Here's a checklist that will help pin down the reason for their task avoidance. As ever, don't guess, ask.

- **Is there a problem with the work?**

Perhaps they've lost confidence in their ability to do the job or to work a new system and they don't want to ask for help. It baffles me why organisations spend fortunes on new systems without earmarking enough money to train people how to use them. D'oh!

- **Is the person neurodivergent?**

Does that person need support or reasonable adjustments? They may struggle with their workload, doing too much screen-based work, need more verbal instructions than written ones, or need to find a quieter, less stimulating place in which to work.

- **Is that person overwhelmed?**

Remember Ellie, our people pleaser in Chapter 8? When there's too much to do, we find it hard to get anything done, because we don't know where to start. We freeze and inertia sets in. These people need to re-clarify the priorities of their role and ensure how they spend their time reflects these priorities. Often, they are trying to please everyone and need to push back. They might also need help in setting boundaries.

- **Are they a procrastinating perfectionist?**

These are whirling dervishes who spin around in busy circles. Their perfectionist tendencies make them nervous of a less than A* performance, without considering if the task is worthy of that much effort. These people procrastinate from fear of failure, and they delay starting tasks until a deadline looms and then they create a bottleneck.

These people comfort themselves with the excuse of lack of time when a result doesn't meet their high standards. They need to cut back on distracting communication channels, set mini deadlines, block out time for tasks and get structure into their week.

- **Is the person bored?**

  Maybe their skills and experience have increased, but their level of responsibility is stuck in a rut. As a result, their performance takes a dive. Extra responsibilities or dealing with challenging curveballs might re-energise them. They need to learn how to handle this transition with more maturity next time.

- **Have they lost motivation?**

  I'm an advocate of Daniel Coyle's view in his bestselling book *The Culture Code* that a leader's job is to hire motivated people and inspire them. In our volatile world, it is easy to lose sight of what's genuinely important. Why not discuss what matters to a team member who seems lazy and unengaged? Have a chat about why they do their job and who benefits from their work.

  In my first book *Mind Flip: Take the Fear out of Your Career,* I explain that work is more fulfilling when we focus on what we do for others, and the problems we uniquely solve for them, rather than being consumed by our own issues. You can help someone to find a renewed sense of purpose.

- **Are they struggling with mental ill-health?**

  Depression and anxiety can lead to lethargy and a loss of interest and pride in work. Perhaps they are worried about something in their personal life. This demands gentle handling and specialist support. They may need a reduced workload while rebuilding their self-esteem and confidence. I once coached someone whose father had recently died. Her manager told her to throw herself into work to take her mind off it. This crass comment had the opposite effect.

- **Is this person's behaviour a passive-aggressive response to how they are being managed?**

  Have autocratic managers sucked motivation from a colleague by dictating exactly what they should do, or by monitoring their work excessively? People resent being micro-managed and want to think for themselves. Taking this away from them shifts them into a playful or resentful child ego state; they mess around and see what they get away with.

When someone's performance slips, the instinct is to micro-manage them even more, often making the problem worse. The best option is an adult-to-adult discussion to break the behavioural spiral and prompt someone to take more responsibility about their performance.

These reasons apply to people whose performance has tailed off, rather than people who began their role as lazy. Let's hope these are weeded out during their probationary period. They should be set free to do something else, for their own good and everyone else's. The decision to let them go is even easier if they are rude or refuse constructive feedback.

What steps should Remi take?

My client Remi was a peer of Dylan's, in a team of three reporting to Alistair. It's unlikely that Alistair had been coached in how to divide his time between his own tasks and supporting his young team: another *'accidental manager'*.

Managing his work/life balance was the only skill where Dylan seemed to *shine,* although Alistair failed to notice this. He held unstructured and unchallenging one-to-one sessions with Remi. It was likely he was managing Dylan in a similar ineffective way, oblivious of Dylan's daily activity.

We discussed Remi's options.

1 Play the long game. Do nothing and see what happens. The standard of her work would likely be noticed and rewarded by senior management. And Dylan might leave.
2 Tackle Dylan about his behaviour.
3 Broach the problem with Alistair.

Option one, which boils down to keeping calm and carrying on, wouldn't work. Remi was fizzing with resentment.

She'd tried option two. Remi said talking to Dylan got her nowhere. He'd told her to 'chill out and not be so intense' last time she tried to tackle the issue. She was so frustrated that she could barely look at him. Withdrawing made her look moody, turning her into the 'difficult' one.

She had to go for option three.

Remi had moved into classic child ego state on the parent–adult–child model I described in Kumar's story in Chapter 7. Her own behaviour with Dylan had become passive-aggressive; she felt out of control and helpless. What she needed was to shift back into an adult ego state and flag the problem with Alistair professionally. The longer she buried it, the more she enabled Dylan's behaviour.

I asked why Remi had let the problem get this far without talking to Alistair.

Conflict avoidance – individual level

Remi explained that her natural response to conflict was to avoid it – child ego state behaviour. She was worried about the fall-out from speaking up, that she might be judged negatively for it. Psychotherapist Philippa Perry says conflict avoidance is akin to people pleasing. It stems from the same fear of hurting people should you state your needs. Remi was brought up in a home where tough conversations never happened from fear of upsetting her volatile grandparents, who lived with Remi and her parents. Remi created a belief that she would be rejected if she rocked the boat.

Researchers David Watson and Ronald Friend describe conflict avoidance as fear of negative evaluation (FNE). People who score high on their FNE scale are anxious about social approval and have a desperate need to conform. This can result in people becoming submissive, neglecting healthy boundaries and sacrificing their own needs to please others.

Conflict avoidance – systemic level

When workplace conflict remains unresolved, individuals like Remi tend to feel more and more resentful. It also gives rise to broader cultural issues such as decreased problem-solving and collaboration, while increasing distrust. Problems should be raised and dealt with sensitively.

Conflict between people is normal. Handling it with respect and a professional attitude creates better performance. Harvard Business School's Amy Edmondson's concept of psychological safety is sometimes misread as 'are you OK, hon?' But Edmondson is calling for the opposite of fluffy throwaway questions that bury issues. She's calling for an environment where people feel it's safe to confront someone. If people don't feel safe, they will change the subject when given an opportunity to speak up.

Ineffective or unpleasant managers remain unchanged until someone flags up their behaviour. When organisations make headlines for toxic behaviour, it exposes a culture of ignoring problems, rather than confronting them. People in power can no longer use ignorance as an excuse.

I knew the culture of Remi's organisation well and could reassure her she'd be safe to have a discreet conversation with Alistair about the unfair division of work.

She calmly explained to him how this was troubling her, without directly criticising Dylan. Alistair asked her how she wanted him to handle it. Whatever his motive for asking this, it was the right approach for Remi, as it boosted her confidence in resolving her problem. We'd already discussed this, so she presented her plan, suggested making the most of their project management software, rather than continuing to use it haphazardly. Alistair would assign tasks fairly to all three team members and track their progress, dividing work and tracking progress through the tasks. It would make everything more transparent.

Alistair followed Remi's suggestion and, during the next couple of months, it became clear who was at full capacity and who wasn't.

He tackled Dylan, who promptly applied for a transfer to another team. Alistair encouraged this. It was an easier option than the more professional but painful one of starting a performance management process. It's often described as passing the turkey, rather than cooking the goose.

Remi grew in confidence. She realised that hard work alone wouldn't make her successful; she had to find her voice too. When another colleague tried to take credit for some work she did, she faced her fear of conflict and raised it with him.

Questions that help you understand why you avoid conflict

- 'What would my life be like without this conflict?'
- 'What would it be like if this conflict continues?'
- 'What's stopping me from dealing with it?'

Resources

Edmondson, A.C. (2018) *The Fearless Organization, Creating Psychological Safety in the Workplace*, Wiley.

Everett, Z. (2020) *Mind Flip: Take the Fear out of Your Career*, Curlew House.

Perry, P. (2023) *The Book You Want Everyone You Love* to Read (and maybe a few you don't)*, Penguin.

Turner, S. and Weed, F. (1983) *Conflict in Organisations*, Prentice Hall Direct.

Watson, D. and Friend, R. (1969) Measurement of social-evaluative anxiety, *Journal of Consulting and Clinical Psychology* 33(4), 448–57.

Chapter 18

I need to speak up more

'Dear Zena

People I work with seem to have no problem speaking up at meetings or voicing their opinions, even when they don't have much to say. It's not in my nature to do this, but I know I need to get my point of view across and get noticed or I won't get on. I also hate networking events; I can't make small talk like everyone else seems to.'

Themes

- Confidence
- Assertiveness
- Personal branding
- Introversion and extraversion
- Networking skills

This was an email I received after I ran a career strategy session in a bank and offered free coaching sessions as part of it.

Teddy was in his second year there, having been hired through a recruitment programme that prioritised under-represented groups. He was a clever, ambitious man, keen to fulfil his potential. He grabbed the opportunity for some coaching. Not everyone likes to reach out for help or is self-aware enough to know when they need it. Ted's behaviour wasn't bad in the usual way, but he realised it was holding him back.

Ted was quiet and thoughtful, unlike some of his louder contemporaries who perhaps enjoyed the sound of their own voice too much. Ted's family had taught him not to speak unless invited to do so. He felt interrupting or talking over someone, particularly someone more senior, showed real disrespect.

If only the rest of us thought before we spoke. But in Ted's alpha dog environment, with colleagues jostling for the next role up, Ted's silence risked being seen as having nothing special to contribute. His 'bad' behaviour was staying quiet. He needed to be more visible, as well as bold enough to speak up.

Ted wasn't short of opinions; he just didn't like to give them unless invited. While it's best practice to ask for everyone's opinions at meetings, this rarely happens. Ted found Teams meetings particularly tricky as people seemed to talk over each other even more than they would in the same room. If he didn't speak, the spotlight shone elsewhere and Ted felt more marginalised. He risked being held back by a glass ceiling of his own making.

This is nothing to do with being an introvert or an extrovert. Extroverts can be shy, and introverts may be the ones dancing on the table. The difference between them is what they do when their energy is drained and in need of a boost. Introverts need some time to themselves, while extroverts seek the company of others.

Ted wanted to stay true to himself, while learning to play the corporate game. This is often called being 'authentic', but I prefer to use 'genuine'. I've seen several situations when 'authenticity' has been commandeered as an excuse for speaking without filtering, as in: 'I tell it like it is. I can't help who I am.' Yes, you can. You can be true to yourself without crossing the line into rudeness or being unkind.

How could Ted become more visible and be heard more without changing who he was?

We talked about the brand he wanted to cultivate – forgive the cliché, but it's important. He needed a point of view, a way of analysing problems that people would recognise as the value he brought to a discussion. He was an economics graduate, very well read and with fast mental processing. He had something to say. He might not be first to speak but when he did, he'd make his points clearly and confidently, so people would listen and take him seriously.

Here's what Ted did to get more authority. Most of his meetings were online, but these tactics apply in person too. As ever, it's about looking approachable and confident, even when you might not feel it.

- He joined meetings bang on time, even early if allowed in, to say hello to the organiser and make a positive impression. Nothing forced, just a light hello and some easy small talk. I'm always grateful to the people who join my online sessions early and look pleased to be there.

- He planned the point he wanted to make, even writing it down if necessary, so he could articulate it confidently when the gap came up to make it. He took his time to say what he needed to get across and, if people tried to interrupt, he practised acknowledging them but kept going. I encouraged him to watch current affairs programmes to see how politicians do this with varying degrees of politeness.

- If he had no extra opinion to contribute, he'd still speak up and say how he agreed with other people's views, maybe summing up the debate input and suggesting an action.

- He kept his camera on and moved a little, even when not speaking – thumbs up, smiling, nodding. Nothing forced or unnatural, just appearing present and interested.

Ted loved clothes. I'd never tell anyone what to spend their money on, but Ted told me he'd dialled up his style to look like the successful banker he aspired to be. It worked wonders for Ted's confidence, and he felt it gave him an edge.

Politicians tend to use clothes and hair to make their mark. Former Chancellor of Germany Angela Merkel – the only woman to hold that office – was known for her distinctive jackets, and former UK Prime Minister Theresa May carved out a reputation as a clothes horse, right down to her fondness for leopard print shoes. And her successor Boris Johnson drew regular media comments for sporting a blond mop of hair that was deliberately messed up to create a 'man of the people' persona. In the late 19th century, American writer and designer Edith Wharton described clothes as functioning as 'armour' for their ability to bestow social advantage and I guess it works today, too.

Small talk and networking events

Ted avoided networking events because he found small talk awkward. Small talk is the vital career skill of chitchatting with a stranger or newish person at a social event, perhaps a more senior person with whom we want to forge a bond.

This skill feels alien to many of us. It's an even worse ordeal for those who are neurodiverse or very introverted and struggle to make direct eye contact. Anyone fortunate enough to have picked up these skills at the family dinner table, or in a collegiate system at university, are more comfortable with formal social situations. It offers a huge career advantage.

I've been in toe curling situations with younger people who have obviously searched online for *Top Networking Tips* and ask weird questions: 'Hello Zena, can you describe a pivotal moment in your career?' This is too eccentric.

The secret is to be yourself, maybe a little more smiley than you feel. 'Hi Zena, lovely to meet you. How are you?' is a perfectly good opener. Look at the person, listen to what they say, ask a question or two – although not the slightly strange type I mentioned earlier – to get them talking, laugh at their jokes and you are off to the races.

My top tip for networking events is to get there early, tempting though it might be to turn up later. It's much easier to strike up a conversation as everyone arrives, instead of having to break into conversations.

➤

> If it helps you to feel more confident, find a purpose for being there. Help the organisers by introducing people to each other or hand out drinks or food at an informal, unstaffed event. Just make sure that you are networking as you do it, not simply beavering away behind the scenes.
>
> I recently spoke at a conference for a manufacturing trade association, with 12 executive committee members: 11 male, one female. At the event's registration, the men were meeting and greeting in the main event hall, working the room. Their female colleague was in the foyer, having volunteered to hand out name badges.
>
> A couple of young women attendees pointed this out to me; they were infuriated that a woman had fallen into this trap, despite making it as a senior player in their male-dominated industry sector.

Resources

Goyder, C. (2014) *Gravitas: Communicate with Confidence, Influence and Authority*, Vermilion.

Wharton, E. (1920) *The Age of Innocence*, Oxford World's Classics.

Chapter 19

I see everything as a problem

'**Dear Zena**

Can you help our new company accountant? Nikki is excellent at transactional work, but she's getting a reputation for being negative and prickly. She often jumps to quick conclusions. Sometimes she's right, but sometimes her thinking is flawed. She won't budge, even when presented with facts that contradict her opinions. She's coming across as an annoying "computer says no" obstacle.'

Themes

- Cognitive distortions
- Confirmation bias
- Cognitive behavioural coaching
- ABC technique of rational beliefs
- Resilience and mental fitness

Nikki was a blatant example of a negative mindset causing negative behaviour.

Cognitive distortions are mental filters that lead to unhelpful and irrational ways of thinking that feed into behaviour. These are the smirking critics inside our heads, making us see the world and ourselves as gloom-ridden.

Our thoughts become a defence mechanism to keep us safe from perceived threats: you're not good enough to handle this, don't risk it! These thoughts are counterproductive, of course. People see our defensive behaviour as pig-headed, troublesome or plain weird. We avoid tackling challenging or new things because our prehistoric brain wants us to stay safe in our cave.

Every fibre in our being warns us not to go near a menace we have twisted into something far too dangerous. We no longer face

woolly mammoths, only tough conversations, or working with new
people who are probably pussycats, working through their own
vulnerabilities.

Nikki was displaying several cognitive distortions.

All-or-nothing thinking

This is black or white thinking, dividing views into opposing
positions, with no grey or nuance in-between. This is people
thinking in extremes, regardless of facts.

* *If we don't hit our budgets, we've failed at everything.*
* *This person can't set up a spreadsheet; they are completely useless.*
* *Salespeople are only interested in commission; they don't care about
the sustainability of the business.*
* *That person looked at their phone once during our meeting. I can't
stand them; they are completely rude and arrogant.*
* *If I'm not in control, everything will all fall apart.*

Overgeneralisation becomes the norm

Sometimes, people expect something negative to happen because of
a previous negative experience. One event becomes a rule for life.
Instead of looking for unbiased evidence, we look for information
that supports our position and ends in confirmation bias.

* *I can't be bothered to train the new accounts assistant. Gen Z
workers never stay longer than six months, so what's the point?*
* *You can't trust managers to run their own P & L.*
* *If a client is a late payer, you can never sell to them again.*
* *Investors are only interested in short-term rewards.*
* *Remote workers never work as hard as office-based workers.*

Discounting the positive

The trap here is dismissing something as of no value, despite clear positive aspects. It's a simple case of seeing the miserable in everything.

- *He said he liked the format of this month's report; so I guess he thought earlier ones weren't good enough?*
- *She smiled at me in the lift this morning; what's going on behind my back?*
- *We had a great last quarter; the clients are probably stockpiling and won't buy anything this quarter. We're doomed.*
- *I got the job; I was probably the cheapest candidate in a bad bunch.*
- *It's the first time everyone is in the office together for ages; they'll spend the day chatting and won't get any work done.*
- *That piece of work was quite easy. I should work harder.*

Can your emotions handle the truth?

The way you feel reflects your reality. If you feel it, you see it as fact. As Ruby Wax, comedian, author and mental health campaigner, says in her book *Sane New World*, you think your emotions are telling you the truth. This thinking particularly infects our social lives.

- *Most people here are younger than me. I don't fit in.*
- *Everyone else here has at least two degrees. I've only got one, so I'm out of my depth and shouldn't be here.*
- *My managing director sometimes does a lift-share with one of my colleagues; I bet they talk about me.*
- *I feel angry; it's the sales team's fault.*

Living your own disaster blockbuster

This is *From Here to Disaster* in one sentence. The one where we over-think and look at the absolute worst case. Perhaps best to avoid watching too many end-of-the-world blockbusters.

- *If I lose this job, I'll never find another one; we'll lose our home and my family will fall apart.*
- *There's talk of a recession; the market is a dead cert to implode and we'll all be doomed.*

These punishing patterns of negative thinking are there to protect us from our core fears. These are what we think deep-down about our right to be here, to belong. To save you years of therapy, these are the most frequent ones:

- *I'm not good enough.*

   This is the most common, garden-variety root fear, and it prompts us to compensate for it.

- *I must please everyone.*
- *I must be perfect.*

Nikki's problem was she was riddled with negative thinking. Yet, assuming the worst about herself and everyone else made her feel more anxious and unhappy. She saw bad behaviour when it didn't exist, and her defensiveness created genuine bad behaviour from others. She lost sleep, all the worry sucked away her energy and made her unable to relax at weekends. None of it was useful in restoring Nikki to balanced thinking or turning up to work with enthusiasm.

   Then she had all the other problems created by this primary problem around her negative thinking pattern. Nikki now had corrosive relationships with colleagues. These escalated her downward spiral at work and lessened her chances of success.

Nikki needed a new way of thinking, one that would 'solve problems, not perpetuate them', as Michael Neenan, Associate Director of the Centre for Stress Management, wrote in his book on cognitive behavioural therapy, *Developing Resilience*.

Cognitive reframing and the move to rational thought

Cognitive behavioural therapy (CBT) unpicks the relationship between our thoughts, feelings and behaviours, moving us into a more rational, positive state of mind. Unlike other therapies, it focuses not on our early lives – since we can't change those – but on our current problems.

It moves our attention from the external world to our internal world, pushing us to reflect on our often-illogical interpretation of events and other people's behaviour. It untangles our twisted thinking and replaces it with thoughts that are easier to live with because they make more sense.

I used a CBT model with Nikki called the ABC model of rational beliefs, created by American psychologist Albert Ellis. I could use it on every client in this book, if it were appropriate and safe to go deep with them.

Nikki and I used it to unpack a recent situation to show Nikki how her thoughts controlled her behaviour. It's not what happens that causes our problems, it's our fundamental beliefs about it. We can challenge and change these.

A – activating event

B – our belief about it

C – our behavioural consequences

Nikki's original A to C thinking

A – activating event (the spark)

Senior sales manager Dave came into the accounts department to talk to Nikki about extending credit facilities to some new customers to enable them to do business.

C – consequences (Nikki's behaviour)

Nikki said no, we can't do this. The company already has a tight cash flow and can't afford the cost of financing the new business if things go wrong. Dave was infuriated. He felt Nikki wasn't listening to him and there ought to be a way to get this new business. Otherwise, he couldn't do his job. He stormed out. Nikki felt stressed and preoccupied for the rest of the day and got little done. Dave had been rude, and she shouldn't have to put up with this.

Nikki's behaviour wasn't caused by A, the activating event. It's caused by B, her belief about it:

B – belief (the thoughts that create the behaviour)

Nikki knew the agency she and Dave worked for wasn't in great shape, but many employees hadn't been told the full story.

The managing director had told her to keep a tight grip on the purse strings – at all costs. Fair enough, but she could have got all the facts from Dave and offered to look for a risk-free way of getting these new customers and their business. Why didn't she? She didn't because of her distorted core beliefs, and you'll see we drilled down to get to her core one, at the end.

- *Dave doesn't understand finance, typical sales.*
- *Dave doesn't understand what I do and doesn't respect me, I'm not helping him.*
- *I must please the MD, so I'll do exactly what she tells me.*
- *I can't figure this out; it's too risky.*
- *I must stay in tight control of the money, or it will be disastrous.*
- *I'm tired and fed up with the stress; I can't do this anymore.*
- *I'm not good enough to be here.*

We discussed this belief that she wasn't good enough to be in her job. There's a touch of imposter syndrome here, covered in more detail in Chapter 16. With Nikki, this was about more than straightforward self-awareness; it was tapping into Nikki's self-defeating belief that she wasn't good enough – full stop.

Changing your beliefs

The next step is to replace this belief with a more rational one. Was it true that she didn't deserve to be in the job, that she wasn't up to it? Of course not. A competent MD had hired her. Nikki was already in the role and was doing okay in the job. Maybe not perfectly and she wasn't in control of everything, but she was unmistakeably doing her job.

It was her behaviour (caused by her beliefs) that was her problem, not her capability.

I asked her:

If you knew you were good enough to be here, what would you do differently?

Nikki said: '*I would act like it. I'd lighten up and stop worrying. I'd walk over to Dave's desk, ask if he had a moment, make us coffee, and explain I was preoccupied with cash flow without divulging too much.*

'*I'd find out more about the credit worthiness of the customer and explore what was possible. Then I'd write a new credit policy. I'd listen to Dave and get to know him. I'll also do that with his peers in the agency, so we understand each other's challenges and build trust.*'

This is A to B thinking instead of A to C, where we get ourselves in-between our thoughts and our reaction to them. Thoughts and feelings aren't facts. In coaching, we deal with facts.

What am I telling myself in this situation? Is that true? If not, what is true?

Nikki and I unpacked similar situations during her year's coaching programme. She taught herself not to take everything so seriously, that everything wasn't on her shoulders because she was part of a team. She learned to breathe before reacting, slowed down, enjoyed the work, smiled at people more and got to know more about them and what was going on.

People learned to trust her more and began using her as a sounding board. She was less anxious, so she took better care of herself, and this fed into her energy levels and mood at work, too.

How to use the ABC model to coach yourself

I take myself through that model whenever I am anxious, usually stressing about doing everything perfectly.

What pressure am I putting on myself?

What do I think will be obvious to everyone else?

These are brilliant questions for getting to the heart of the belief, from Dr Ellen Hendriksen's book *How to Be Yourself*.

I now coach myself to leave my house early, turn up in plenty of time and try to have a good time. This assumes I'm well prepared, which I will have taken care of earlier. Ultimately, that's all I can control.

I may or may not be good enough, but I've got a job to do, so I might as well give it everything I've got.

Warning: working with triggers, trauma and PTSD

A trigger is an emotional response to trauma. Trauma can stem from childhood or domestic abuse, violence, accidents, hate crime or racism, or from witnessing distressing events, such as those experienced by members of the emergency services, military, social or medical professions. They are triggered when something happens that takes their mind and body right back to the traumatic event. People with substance or alcohol abuse disorders can be triggered by situations or people who cause them to feel dangerous cravings.

We use the word 'triggered' casually now when we feel offended or made uncomfortable or angry by something. That's fair enough and more than valid. It's just not the correct use of the word 'triggered' which should only apply to genuine psychological trauma. It's not a word to use lightly, because it minimises the experience of people who need specialist support.

Nikki's bad behaviour was sparked by her conversation with Dave, not triggered. The ABC model worked with her because she had disordered thinking, not post-traumatic stress disorder (PTSD). I wouldn't have attempted working with her if this had been the case.

People with PTSD need specialist support. There's more information on https://www.mind.org.uk/information-support/types-of-mental-health-problems/post-traumatic-stress-disorder-ptsd-and-complex-ptsd/for-friends-and-family/.

Resources

Henriksen, E. (2018) *How to Be Yourself*, St Martin's Press.

Neenan, M. (2009) *Developing Resilience, A Cognitive-Behavioural Approach*, Routledge.

Neenan, M. and Dryden, W. (2002) *Life Coaching, A Cognitive-Behavioural Approach*, Routledge.

Wax, R. (2013) *Sane New World: Taming the Mind*, Hodder & Stoughton.

Chapter 20

I'm stuck: everyone is doing better than me

'Dear Zena

I'm stuck in my career. Everyone else is doing better than me and I feel left behind. I don't know what to do next. I'm scared that I'll make a wrong decision and mess up my CV. All my university friends seem to have found careers they are passionate about. Why can't I?'

Themes

- Scrappy careers and contemporary careers theory
- Career decisions
- Career anxiety
- Resilience and mental fitness

Jules's anxiety about making the wrong career decision was stopping her from contributing as much as she could or enjoying the early years of her career. This is another case of bad behaviour coming from good intentions; someone sabotaging their own success and well-being. I see it frequently.

So far, Jules had ticked all the boxes: scholarship to a fantastic school where she got A-grades in everything, along with Grade 8 for violin, made sports team captain and was a keen reader. Then she racked up a first-class degree in languages from an excellent Scottish university where she was a keen debater. She'd won a place on a highly competitive graduate scheme at a top London management consultancy, where she worked as a third-year analyst on a great salary.

Jules had never failed at anything. She was terrified at the idea of failure, even a little. She'd already turned down an opportunity for a secondment to the company's Paris office because she was concerned that she risked missing out on promotion if she was rarely seen in London, where most of the partners were.

But there was no evidence that would happen. In fact, Jules had feedback to the contrary – the partners were surprised she passed on a great opportunity. They'd also noticed her lack of confidence. She resisted tackling projects unless her grasp of the subject was rock solid. Jules struggled with looking confident in front of clients when she wasn't feeling it. Most consultants admit it's an essential skill in their profession.

Jules also worried she had no burning passion for what she did, or that she didn't have a hard-and-fast career plan mapped out.

Instead of going with the flow, she felt she should have a plan. A true north. Her one true path. She thought everyone else had these. Work can be stressful enough without the pressure to 'find a job you love so much you never have to work a day in your life'.

Careers theory used to be all about the importance of a plan. I've lost count of the number of career presentations I've seen that warn of the dangers of drifting into new areas, as if doing so is the worst thing anyone could do. Many warnings include a version of the popular *Alice in Wonderland* white rabbit misquote:

'*If you don't know where you are going, any road will take you there.*'

The trouble is, Lewis Carroll never wrote that. It's from a George Harrison song called *Any Road*.

Jules's parents had sensible career plans. They'd never drifted into anything. They were fortunate to have joined accountancy firms after university and worked their way up, step by step, to partner level. That's what people did in those days: they had fewer options and grabbed opportunities for social mobility. They didn't always have the luxury of questioning their choices.

Career choices are more ambiguous now. It's impossible to have a long-term plan when we can't predict what the future will hold. If we try to hang on to a rigid plan, we risk missing exciting opportunities that can sneak up on us. A rigid plan is the last thing we want.

The jobs people do today didn't exist until recently. Space cadet used to be an insult, but now it's a realistic job option. Ten years ago no one had titles like crypto engineer, autonomous vehicle designer, app developer, content creator, cultivated meat farmer or big data analyst.

According to a report published by Dell Technologies and authored by the **Institute for the Future** (IFTF) together with technology, business and academic experts from around the world, 85 per cent of the jobs that will exist in 2030 have yet to be created.

This volatility has flipped career strategy to encouraging a far more experimental and fun approach. Herminia Ibarra, the Charles Handy Professor of Organisational Behaviour at London Business School, wrote about shifting from 'plan and implement' to 'doing and reviewing' in her seminal career book *Working Identities*. Our ability to keep up with the pace of change and gain new knowledge is almost more desirable than the knowledge itself.

When career coaching, I always ask the client who is influencing their decisions. They frequently have an inner critical voice. Whose voice is it?

You don't need to be Sigmund Freud to work out that Jules was worried about letting down her parents. She'd been successful at everything she'd done in her young life so far; she felt a failure for wanting to move on from her prestigious employer. She'd never failed at anything before and so, taking that chance and risking failure was a really big deal.

We explored this with some sensible questions you'll probably recognise by now.

Is that true? Would you be letting your parents down if you made a change?

She said her parents only wanted her to be happy, of course, and they'd support any decision she made. We talked about the dangers of career comparisons and how people's LinkedIn and Instagram profiles don't always reflect the realities of their daily lives. Swiss-born British author, public speaker and philosopher Alain de Botton believes we are all 'job snobs' now. We judge people by their job title, commonly with envy and some comparison with our own job, but we're usually imagining the underlying picture. Some of these job titles also seem created to obscure the reality of the job.

Our perception of career and life success comes from many sources: our parents' expectation, our peers, colleagues, classmates, neighbours, friends. We benchmark our extrinsic success against theirs; where we think we '*should*' be.

How you spend your days should fit your values and priorities – no one else's. If you work part time to take care of your family, that's fine. If you are the parent who rarely does school pickup, that's fine too. Some people give up corporate life to take a risk. Others stay on the corporate track because they like the security. Everyone can choose what suits their life.

Whole-heartedly do what feels right for you now, and you can always change later. Jules wanted to change, but was anxious about making the perfect choice.

I explained to her that careers are now seen as a series of stages, some of them in work, some away from work to take on caring responsibilities or renewed studying. These stages might mean taking lateral moves in search of deep expertise, straight-up moves, or taking time out to do something radically different. There are many twists and turns instead of a straight line. The last time I looked we can expect at least eight or nine steps in our sequences. You have probably had several pivots and reinventions yourself; I have and hope I have more left in me.

Scrappy careers – the way to see a safe path

We can remove the pressure if we see each career stage as a patch of safe ground where we accumulate as many skills, networks and experiences as possible. Once we've outgrown a stage, we can move on to the next patch of safe ground. We keep doing this and usually can't see more than a couple of patches ahead, but we aren't worried about that. As we move, the fog clears, and we can see a little further ahead. What's important is that we keep moving, learning and enjoying ourselves.

It's a more scrappy, entrepreneurial approach to work. We make the most of where we are, contributing as much as we can, then move on when the time is right and take our skills elsewhere. We may go back to previous employers once we have accumulated extra experience, something they might find valuable. That's a far better approach than being stale and underproductive because we've outgrown our role.

As the saying goes, our vibe is our tribe. We build networks and that's where opportunities come from. Even if you get a role through a recruiter, chances are someone in your network has given them your name or a reference. The one thing that hasn't changed is that it's who you know that matters most. We often underestimate the value of our networks for offering opportunities and vital feedback.

Jules listed everything she brought to the table. Everything! Every functional and technical skill, software package, language, customer knowledge, relationship, interest and network. We talked about when she was happiest at work, the teams, managers and tasks she found most enjoyable.

I've said that not everyone has found a calling or North Star, despite all the books and videos that tell us how to do it. Some never do. But we need to find a sense of purpose, where we get our meaning and sense of well-being from. Why do we get up in the morning?

I asked Jules the following question.

If you made a change, how would you know in a year's time that you had made the right decision? What would you feel like?

Jules said working in a supportive, sociable team was most important to her. She would know she had made the right decision if she looked forward to going into the office to see her colleagues. Travel would be excellent too.

It turned out that what worried her most about her job was the culture, not the work itself. She worked for a ruthlessly competitive firm, straight out of a John Grisham novel. Colleagues scored each other at the end of each project and she felt she was competing with them for career-enhancing assignments. Management wasn't particularly supportive and changed from one assignment to another. She had a mentor, who mostly talked about themselves and showed little interest in her. She felt isolated and unsupported.

I took her back a step, to double-check that this wasn't a confidence issue.

If you knew you'd be super successful at this role, what would your decision be?

Jules knew she could do the work successfully, but said she didn't fit with the firm's culture and environment. She was happy to work long hours and handle the client pressure; her high salary was her reward. But she wanted a team culture with kinder, more caring people and she wanted to feel a part of something. She felt a culture where people were permanently on edge rarely got the best from most people. It might be good for lone wolves, but not for team players like her. Her values were different from theirs and that's usually the end of the road.

That was all she needed to decide to move. Even though she wasn't sure if management consultancy was the long-term career for her, she wanted to go somewhere else where she would be happier. Her company was an illustrious name to have on her CV and it was a useful place to use as a pivot, in search of her next patch of safe ground.

Jules put out feelers to specialist management consultancy recruiters. She went to a smaller firm, set up by previous partners from her large, existing one, one of which she'd worked with when she first joined. They did the same client work, but in a more collegiate way. They'd built a supportive team culture.

Jules' immediate goal was to work hard and get a deposit for a flat. She told me she might work for one of her clients in the future if she wanted to trade off the high compensation and travel for more flexibility and balance. Another option was to do a part-time master's degree, maybe with a contribution from the firm. She even wondered if she might go back to her first employer in a more senior role, where she would have the chance to influence the corporate culture. For now, she was enjoying her safe patch of ground.

These are useful questions to help people who feel stuck in their career:

- Why do you do what you do?
- Whose opinion about your career do you most consider? Is that helpful? Are they right?
- When were you happiest at work? What were you doing? Why did you do it and what was the context? Who were you working with and did that make a difference?
- What skills, knowledge, networks and personal experiences do you bring to the table?
- What did you enjoy doing most when you were younger and why?
- If you knew that you'd be super successful at whatever you did next, what would your first step be?

Career transitions

Some people genuinely have a vocation or calling, perhaps one they found when they were young. I often ask people who are stuck in their career what they enjoyed doing most as a child. Many of us seem to loop back to this eventually, or at least incorporate that interest into our lives, even if it's not the main area of how we earn a living.

Pop singer from the 1980s Alison Moyet has graduated recently with a degree in her first love, fine art printmaking. More recent singer Adele has announced a plan to follow her passion for English Literature by taking a degree in it. Dave Rowntree, former drummer for pop group Blur, has announced a plan to stand for election to the UK Parliament as a Labour party MP.

When a client is weighing up career options, the 'crazy option' that they mention last is often the one that they would most like to do. If their circumstances don't permit them to do it full-time, I encourage them to experiment as a side project and see if it eventually takes over. Total career pivots are unusual, despite how people portray them in the media: 'I was a lawyer, now I'm a celebrity florist.' Usually there is a long period of overlap and many hours of hard work before people make radical transitions.

Don't worry if you haven't yet found your 'path'. Like life partners, there's more than one option for everyone and plenty of time to get it right. Just do your best and make the most of your patch of safe ground.

If you feel frustrated that your job is meeting your financial needs for now, and circumstances rule out a change right now, just accept it. This is a common mid-career funk, living for the big pot at the end of the career rainbow . . . once the children are through school . . . or you cash in when the business is sold . . . and so on. You may feel that your motivation has fallen compared with how pumped you felt earlier in your career.

Keep your eyes on your long-term prize while finding satisfying short-term milestones and targets – maybe a challenging side project. Real life is lived day to day, not in the big moments. Change your focus to daily achievements to get your energy restored. Find pockets of whatever it takes to make your day a good one: intellectual stimulation, deep work, challenges, validation, appreciation, successful collaborations, rewarding tasks, inspiring bosses, thankful customers, new skills, creative challenges, problem-solving or maybe a long walk at the end of the day. Maybe just some time to kick back and read a book.

Make repetitive steps in a direction that feels right to you. A solid clue on what's right for you is when you feel most energetic. What's the difference between a good and a bad day? How can you tackle more energising activities and less of the dull ones?

Keep expanding your network, look for opportunities that allow you to learn new skills. Build your networks and find fulfilment in activities and relationships outside of work for now. Take your time. You aren't in a competition.

Resources

de Botton, A. (2005) *Status Anxiety*, Penguin.

Dell.com: Realizing 2030: Dell Technologies Research Explores the Next Era of Human-Machine Partnerships.

Everett, Z. (2020) *Mind Flip: Take the Fear out of Your Career*, Curlew House.

Ibarra, H. (2004) *Working Identity: Unconventional Strategies for Reinventing Your Career*, Harvard Business Review Press.

Chapter 21

Negative colleagues drag me down

'Dear Zena

I love my job, but there are some negative people in my team who complain about everything. I'm a naturally upbeat person, but these daily melodramas knock the stuffing out of me. I can't escape them because of the type of work we do. How can I survive these mood hoovers?'

Themes

- Social contagion
- Difficult people
- Psychological safety

David Brooks, *New York Times* columnist and bestselling author, has written that humans are not just rational beings, but social animals for whom forging emotional connections with others is critical for survival and well-being. These emotions allow us to 'interpenetrate' with each other in ways that reason does not.

Imagine dragging yourself to the gym at the end of a tough day. You open the door to pumping music, warm lighting, friendly receptionists and smiling instructors. Everyone is chatting away, happy to be there and pleased to see you. Your mood brightens and you are glad you made the effort. You've been interpenetrated, lucky you.

You've just experienced social contagion: the spontaneous transfer of emotions between us. The connections we have with other people profoundly impact our thinking, behaviour, relationships, politics, ideas and well-being.

It's not just our immediate network we have to watch out for. Scientists Nicholas Christakis and James Fowler describe the profound power of social networks in their book *Connected*. Their research shows that not only are people surrounded by cheerful people more likely to be cheerful, but the relationship between people's happiness extends up to three degrees of separation – the friends of one's friends' friends. The same applies to health choices, politics, ideas and so on. Your colleague's husband's sister can make you fat, even if you don't know her.

Junior designer Jess was experiencing the power of social contagion, but not in a good way. She worked in a team of three in a small marketing agency. The other designers had been there for much longer and no longer seemed to enjoy the job. One, let's call her Maria, was grumpy and barely said hello in the mornings when they were in the office together. She complained about the clients, the owner of the business, the government, the news, the weather, her husband – pretty much everything was a problem to her.

The other one, Judy, wasn't as bad, but wasn't exactly inspiring. As well as nodding to Maria's complaints, Judy took things personally. Jess found it difficult to ask for clarity on a brief because Judy assumed Jess was criticising her original explanation.

Judy was perhaps being infected by Maria's gloom. Whatever was going on, Jess didn't want to end up like them.

What was she to do? Smile at Maria and hope she'd smile back? Give positive feedback and praise to win her round. Be a conduit for good vibes? Divide and conquer – working on Judy first?

Maybe.

Will Felps studies organisational behaviour at the University of New South Wales and I came across his work in Daniel Coyle's *The Culture Code*. He did an extraordinary experiment by planting Nick, a 'bad apple', into various teams. Nick was alternatively a jerk, a slacker or a miserable, tired downer. Each time, he brought down the team's performance by 30 to 40 per cent. Just like Maria.

However, there was one team where Nick had no impact because they had an outlier: a positive mood booster on the team. He was warm, a listener and a questioner. He brought others back into the conversation. Somehow, he used his inclusivity, his mood and body language to deflect Nick's activity. He wasn't loud or dominant, but he created the conditions for others to perform. They felt safe and connected. As we've already seen, psychological safety – that feeling of being safe and connected – is essential to performance and well-being.

Could Jess be a positive booster like this, to change the culture? Maybe she could, but it would have taken superhuman effort to deflect the atmosphere created by her two older and more experienced colleagues.

And why should she, at her young career stage? She needed training and developing, working with people who'd have a positive influence. It's normal to need to feel safe and supported to thrive.

I asked Jess why she had been put into that team. It felt she'd been left to her own devices, isolated from other team members apart from her immediate colleagues Judy and Maria, and neglected by laissez-faire managers.

It emerged that her parents, who were funding our coaching, had introduced her to the founder of the firm, a supplier to one of their businesses, who had snapped her up.

Externally, his messaging was great, and that's why Jess's parents used his firm and were delighted when she got her job. Clients are the lifeblood of this business, the website declared. Behind closed doors, this commitment was nowhere to be found. A cynical attitude to the clients permeated the company. Apart from an insistence on everyone being in the office at least three days a week, there was little leadership input. People just got on with it. The fish rots from the top and the leader's behaviour is the most contagious. The senior people were good at running a financially sound business but put no effort into the people they employed.

Jess packed up her A-game, put herself on the market and quickly found another job with a much bigger competitor. When she resigned, the managing director appeared shocked and offered her a pay rise to stay. It was too late and her departure wasn't about the money, anyway.

Check to see who dominates the mood – them or you?

If you notice repeating negativity like this, ask yourself:

- *Has this happened to me before?*
- *How do my moods and behaviour affect others?*
- *What can I do differently?*

You may need to get some feedback from people you trust.

Who do you surround yourself with?

How does your network influence you? Are you drained by Negative Marias or fuelled by Sparky Jesses?

Neuroscientist Tara Swart does a great people tree exercise in her book *The Source*. Write down the name of one person you spend time with professionally, then write five words that describe that person – negative or positive, whatever comes to mind. Repeat for another five or so people, then look at the words you've written.

What impact do these people have on you?

How do you feel after spending time with them? What does that tell you?

Would you describe yourself in the same way?

Should you increase or lessen the time you spend with them?

Resources

Brooks, D. (2nd edition, 2012) *Social Animal: A Story of how Success Happens*, Short Books.

Christakis, N. and Fowler, J. (2011) *Connected: The Surprising Power of Our Social Networks and How They Shape Our Lives*, Little, Brown Spark.

Felps, W., Mitchell, T. and Byington, E. (2006) How, when and why bad apples spoil the barrel: negative group member and dysfunctional groups, *Research in Organisational Behaviour* 27, 175–222. Quoted in Daniel Coyle (2018), *The Culture Code*, Random House Business.

Hatfield, E., Cacioppo, J. and Rapson, R. (1994) *Emotional Contagion: Studies in Emotion and Social Interaction*, Cambridge University Press.

Kravetz, L.D. (2017) *Strange Contagion: Inside the Surprising Science of Infectious Behaviors and Viral Emotions and What They Tell Us About Ourselves*, Harper.

Swart, T. (2019) *The Source: Open Your Mind, Change Your Life*, Vermilion.

Changing behaviour

Chapter 22

—

How to behave better

You've now met many of the characters that people my professional life. I daresay you'll have thought of the ones that have already popped up in your working life; you may even have realised that one or two feel suspiciously like yourself. The big question is: what can we learn from these people and their behavioural problems?

These are the life lessons that will help you strengthen your work relationships, manage your own behaviour, maintain your well-being and, most importantly, not drive yourself or others crazy.

1 **You are in command of your own behaviour.**

Even when you feel anxious, angry or vulnerable, you are still in control of what you say and do. The only reason for claiming otherwise is a chronic mental disorder like schizophrenia. Even then, excellent treatments are readily available to help you control your behaviour.

2 **You don't need to act from the power of your feelings.**

Cognitive behavioural techniques teach us to manage how we think and act. Neuroscience has proved that we can change our neural pathways – our thoughts – by consistently acting differently. It's normal to feel anxious sometimes, but that shouldn't restrict your life.

You can plan a strategy to cope in a worst-case scenario and then work out how to mitigate the chances of it happening. It takes practise to get in-between your thoughts and feelings – a stress trigger and your response to it – but it gets easier with practice. Build your resilience by drawing on your experience of coping in other stressful situations. You can do it. Don't let runaway thoughts control you. You will be okay. You just need to remember you are in the driving seat.

3 **Take pride in what you do and take yourself seriously.**

Others treat us as we treat ourselves. Act according to the demands and professional standards of your job description. Be the adult in the room. Decide the reputation you want to build, find a role model and mentor if you can, and behave like that person.

Lack of self-awareness is unattractive, and so is self-deprecation. Putting yourself down is not cute. They may seem useful defence mechanisms, but both will come back to bite you. Being genuine is not the same as feeling pressured to share every aspect of your personal life: put some boundaries between work and home.

If your job is to manage people, then behave like a high-performing manager, not their buddy or caregiver. Ask what they need from you and say what you need from them. Reinvent yourself as you progress in your career.

Consider how an outstanding performer would behave in the job you are in, or aspire to the next level and act the way you would in that role. Even if you don't always feel positive, your mood will catch up with your professional behaviour.

4 **Be consistently pleasant in your dealings with people.**

This is the minimum standard you should aim for. Consistency builds trust and emotional safety. When people don't know how you will respond to them, or feel they need to predict your mood, they become hypervigilant and start treading on eggshells.

That's not the way to build the emotional security people need for productive work relationships. You also risk being excluded and may miss essential information for fear of upsetting you with 'bad news'.

5 **Stop comparing yourself to others.**

LinkedIn profiles are curated. You don't know anyone's starting point, their values or what's really going on in their heads and their lives. You are unique, with your own mix of skills, experience, cultural heritage, qualifications, functional knowledge and networks. Rein in that critical inner voice and stop it from beating you up; focus instead on the contribution you make and the problems you can solve for others. Be the best version of yourself and enjoy being that person.

6 **Be accountable.**

Take responsibility for your behaviour. Own your mistakes. You are human; we all slip up now and then. Admit what you've done, apologise if your mistake has impacted others negatively, change your behaviour and move on.

An apology is pointless without behaviour change. Use a RACI structure – responsible, accountable, consulted, informed – or similar for all your projects so everyone is equally accountable. Know your responsibilities and those that belong elsewhere.

7 **Slow down.**

It's easy to cause offence in the moment, or through a hastily written email or message. Try to sleep on emails before you send them, particularly the sensitive ones. Busyness crowds out genuine communication: allow time to build trust with people.

Take a few minutes to ask people how they are and listen fully to what they say. Eat and drink with colleagues and get to know each other better. It is much easier to solve problems when you have already found some common ground.

Don't overreact when stressed and rushed. Think before you speak. You can press pause on tough conversations; ask for a break and time to reflect. Slow projects down if you need to get extra opinions and support you need before committing to action, or you'll end up rewinding and starting over, creating unnecessary delay.

8 Don't believe your own bullshit, whether it's positive or negative.

Stay humble. Get reality checks and feedback on your blind spots and challenge your own negative thinking. Instead of believing the snarky voices in your head, cultivate a strong, mutually supportive network of people who have your back, people who will give you sensitive but honest feedback.

Is your perception of events the authentic version? Ask them: What am I missing here? Ensure you have people in your network who have a different world view: if you don't, you'll be working in an echo-chamber, not in reality. I have people in my network 20 years younger than me and who I call for their perspectives and vice versa.

9 Know that you can't please everyone.

You will disappoint people from time to time; it's nothing to be ashamed of. Understand who you need to satisfy and when to push back on occasions when time and energy are limited. Learn how to do this professionally, without causing offence.

If you handle this well, the relationship will become stronger. Catch yourself when you try to soothe people to keep on their good side, otherwise known as 'fawning'. You may have felt compelled to do this as a child, but you don't have to do this as an adult. If you can't avoid this, distance yourself from people who make you feel fawning is a necessity; they aren't healthy to have in your life.

10 Remember that you can't rescue people.

Rescuers take excessive responsibility for the emotions and behaviours of others, preventing those people from learning to fix their own problems. You don't need to stop other people feeling discomfort, and they won't thank you for it in the long term.

Influence them positively by being an aspirational, cheerful person to be around. Help them manage their anxiety. Show them you are comfortable with not always having a full picture when making decisions. An action that fails is usually better than not acting at all.

11 Recognise when to give instructions and when to listen.

Most people don't need or want your advice; they want to be heard and to feel validated. They'll be forever grateful if you help them figure out their own answers by you asking great questions and giving them space to think. It's the real route to them learning new behaviour. Chip in with your insights only if necessary. If not, leave it. This is potent soft power: the ability to bring people with you rather than pushing or coercing them by telling them what to do.

12 Understand that not everyone is like you.

No one thinks exactly like you, behaves like you, makes similar decisions or shares your values and approach to life. Not everyone has to like you either. Don't waste energy being frustrated by them or trying to change them or expecting them to be clones of you. All you can change is how you interact with them, responding to their behaviour with sensitivity and professionalism. By all means, develop influencing skills to persuade people to see your point of view, but ultimately it is their choice whether they decide to. Don't judge them either. Be kind.

13 Fly with eagles, don't scratch with turkeys.

Surround yourself with positive and aspirational people who bring out the best in you. Fish rot from the top, so work for the best leader you can. They will be fallible, of course, but they should share the same values as you and create psychological safety so you can thrive in their team. Culture is what people do when no one is looking: scrutinise any discrepancy between what they claim to do and what really happens. Don't feel you have to suck up destructive behaviour: other options exist if you look for them. Don't underestimate the incremental damage to your self-esteem from bad bosses grinding you down.

14 Avoid control freakery.

Things won't fall apart if you're not in control of them. Control freaks don't trust others to do a good job, so they become a bottleneck, checking unnecessary detail and work that's below their pay grade. Learn to trust others. Build in systems so you can check progress if that's needed, then stay in your lane and contribute at your highest level. A good question that will help you prioritise is: 'What is it that only I can do?' Let things go that don't matter.

15 Ditch perfectionism.

Life isn't perfect, decisions won't be perfect, and you aren't perfect either. Few tasks deserve a perfect performance, so don't over-think them or procrastinate. The excessive, unrealistic expectation of giving 100 per cent to everything should be banned. Save your energy for the 10 per cent that really needs maximum effort and attention. Go for those tasks wholeheartedly, all guns blazing. Otherwise, get your tasks completed and passed along to the people waiting for them.

You are good enough; you don't have to prove yourself on every task to show you deserve to be there – you'll be doing the opposite. Don't finesse jobs and constantly add value that isn't needed, you are wasting precious time. Find something more interesting to do. Stop beating yourself up and set an intention to enjoy yourself more. If you do, you'll be far easier to work with.

16 Nip problems in the bud.

Conflict rarely explodes without warning; it's probably been building up. Why let problems fester when prevention is better? Listen to your instincts. Say you've noticed something's adrift and ask the person what's going on; clear the air. Don't assume you know someone else's problem. Ask them. Listen without judgement and discover both sides of the story. This is always best done in person, not by text or email.

17 Above all, understand that life's not fair.

Bad stuff happens to good people. You can't control life's trials. Just go with them when they appear. Cultivate a flexible attitude, rather than rigid expectations. Try to seize opportunities as they occur, even if they weren't in your plan. Enjoy the moment. Don't catastrophise or fall prey to other cognitive distortions.

Catch yourself going down that rabbit hole of over-thinking or other irrational, exaggerated thought patterns. Negative events and bad days do not lead to absolute disasters. Although, in saying this, I'm assuming that most of my readers aren't conducting lifesaving surgery daily. For most of us, a bad day is simply a bad day. Even then, it's still forward momentum. It's work, keep it in perspective. It's called work because it's not play. Work can be tedious or stressful, or both at the same time. You can tolerate that. We all fail sometimes, and that's how we improve. Find healthy coping strategies to distract yourself and come back refreshed the next day.

Strong relationships are governed by boundaries. These are so crucial in eradicating bad behaviour that they've got their own chapter – coming next . . .

Chapter 23

Boundaries: what's your problem and what's not

Boundaries are the limits we set on our relationships to respect the feelings of others and to preserve our own well-being. You wouldn't let your neighbours dump their rubbish in your garden, so why would you let someone do any of the following?

- Dump their workload on you.
- Consistently talk over you or not listen to you.
- Interrupt your private life with unnecessary demands.
- Take credit for your work.
- Criticise you unfairly, speak to you harshly or scold you in public.
- Gossip about you.
- Interfere with your work or monitor your work unnecessarily.
- Speak aggressively to you.

- Ignore you by not responding appropriately.
- Disrespect your physical boundaries.
- Intimidate, harass, victimise or discriminate against you.
- Fail to treat you with dignity and equality or respect your protected characteristics.

These are boundary infringements: people have crossed the line, usually because they don't know where it is.

Some are illegal infringements. It is against UK law to discriminate against someone because of these protected characteristics:

- Age
- Marital status
- Pregnancy or for having a child
- Disability
- Sex, gender reassignment or sexual orientation
- Religious belief or lack of religious belief
- Race, colour and ethnic or national origin

We can't stop others behaving badly, but we can be clear about what we are prepared to tolerate. This is a boundary.

What we believe about ourselves governs how well we do this. If we think we don't deserve respect, then it's likely we won't get it. When we believe we deserve respect, we'll state our limits professionally.

How to enforce professional boundaries

1 Role clarity.

This is knowing what your swim lane is and sticking to it. Be clear on the expectations of your role and how you'll be measured. It sounds obvious, but there can be ambiguity when you have been in an organisation for a long time and have accumulated multiple extra responsibilities.

If you report to several people, whose opinion matters most? Write a one-page updated role description and get it approved. Once you know what your job looks like, you can prioritise, choose or decline curveballs wisely, and know the boundaries you can set around your time and energy. What should you do and what should you stop doing?

2 Know which problems are yours to handle, and which aren't.

The golden rule for boundary setting is treating people with the respect we want for ourselves. However, you can't control anyone's reactions. It's not your job to manage other people's moods. Don't withhold information because you are worried about how the other person will react. You are enabling inappropriate behaviour if you offer kid-glove treatment because you are worried about their reaction.

3 Ask for what you want and stick to it.

Be open and direct about your boundaries, stating what you need, what you can do and when you can do it. Set RACIs, so all accountability is clear. None of us is a mind reader, so mention how you want to operate: 'I'm logging off at 4pm to collect my children. I'll be online again between 8 and 9pm, so please expect a reply then.' Stick to your rules. If you work a four-day week, don't routinely email on day five.

4 Explain what you don't want.

Act like a confident top performer in your current role, or even the one you want next. Decline tasks that don't fit with your priorities, nor those of the person to whom you report. If someone infringes one or more of your boundaries, have a private and professional conversation with them. State the problem clearly and ask for what you want. Ask for their perspective and untangle any crossed wires. If they continue to cross the line, do something about it. Decide what your next step is and get the support and advice you need.

5 Stay professional.

Use the parent–adult–child model from Chapter 7 and stay in the adult ego state that fits your professional status. Colleagues should be able to meet you there, in a rational way. Don't manipulate, plead or make assumptions: stick to the facts. Neither of you needs to act like two overgrown toddlers with unresolved psychological disturbance. You are two adult professionals looking for professional results. While you can't change someone else's behaviour, if you are respectful to them, they'll usually respond with respect. You'll find a workable compromise to move forward productively.

6 Get comfortable with discomfort.

It may feel uncomfortable to set boundaries, especially if you are used to putting other people's needs before your own. You may have experienced rejection when setting boundaries in the past. If you want to press on with asking for something, accept this may make you anxious when having these tough conversations. Accept that discomfort and breathe through it. You are in control of anything that's not worth raising and what's worth standing up for.

7 Understand that sometimes they won't like it.

Occasionally, setting a boundary will make people angry. These are the people who have benefitted from your lack of them. If they respond angrily, it is only because you are no longer bending to their will. Don't capitulate. Their reaction may fade. If it doesn't, it's best to limit contact with them.

If you feel you are treading on eggshells around a person and struggling to set professional boundaries, then you may be dealing with narcissistic behaviour. Please get support. There is no excuse for abusive behaviour.

Chapter 24

The rise of professional coaching

This final chapter looks under the bonnet of the coaching profession.

Coaching done well is the essence of soft power. It gently course-corrects malfunctioning behaviour in a way that makes the other person feel better about themselves. How many people do you know who can do that? Or who can supress their own egos to allow others to thrive? Here's some context if you are hiring a coach or training to be one. As in any transaction, buyer beware.

Having a coach used to be viewed as a remedial intervention in every field other than sport. You only got a coach if you had or were a problem. This changed in 2009 when Eric Schmidt, then CEO of Google and now chair of Alphabet, said in an interview with *Fortune* magazine that the best advice he'd ever been given was to get a coach. He'd hired Bill Campbell, a former college football player and coach, and sales superstar. Campbell's input was revered in Silicon Valley. He went on a weekly Sunday walk with Steve Jobs. Schmidt and the other Google founders said they wouldn't have achieved their success without him.

It became a badge of honour for high achievers to keep a retained coach on speed-dial like this. The pace of change in organisations was and is still frenetic. Coaching provides a safe and structured environment where people can pause, consider the demands they face and perhaps raise the bar on their aspirations. It helps them to feel in control, and to make sense of the world and their place in it. It stops people being distracted by their own story and helps them become more aware of their behaviour. As you've seen, it can be transformational. Anne Scoular, former diplomat and banker, and founder of coaching training company Meyler Campbell, wrote that good coaching is so powerful that if it were a drug, it would be illegal.

Coaching has become a universal form of personal development, not just for the C-suite, but as an investment made at all levels. When managers understand their success relies on making others successful, they often learn how to coach so they can better support their teams.

We're all at it

Name the need and there'll be a coach to meet it: leadership, business, performance, career, redundancy, success, team, life, health, mindset, prosperity, entrepreneurship, nutrition, emotional intelligence, sex, inclusivity, wellness, fitness, public speaking, positivity, accountability, style, confidence, mental health, impact, spiritual, sales, mindfulness, intuitive, finance, business and wealth. We coach individuals, teams and entire companies.

Now that we are used to operating virtually, it's an international marketplace. I know coaches who prefer to stay local: they will only coach when walking outdoors with clients. Whatever works, even in the British winter.

The International Coaching Federation (ICF) estimates the existing global coaching market size exceeds 100,000 practitioners, a 54 per cent increase on the 2019 estimate. The number of coach practitioners has grown in all regions, most notably in the emerging markets of Asia (up by 86 per cent), the Middle East and Africa (up by 74 per cent) and Eastern Europe (up by 59 per cent). The IFC estimated annual income/revenue from coaching of US $4.564 billion, a 60 per cent increase above the 2019 estimate because of the increase in practitioners.

It's questionable how many coaches earn a full-time living from it. For many, it's a side hustle or part of a portfolio of related consultancy services. Globally, more than one in two coaches (53 per cent) reported less than US $30,000 annual income from their practice.

Those ICF numbers are the tip of the iceberg. There are countless coaches who aren't on their radar. These will have paid for a short unaccredited coaching course and set themselves up in business.

The coaches who arguably earn the most and have the highest profiles are those who coach other coaches. Los Angeles- and London-based Rich Litvin is at the top of this pyramid. He describes himself as 'one of the world's most exclusive success coaches'. *The Prosperous Coach*, the book he co-authored with Steve Chandler, has sold more than 70,000 copies and has been in the top 20 books on coaching on Amazon for seven years.

Litvin's website says he leads a community of almost 20,000 coaches and consultants. His training programme divides coaches into four levels: amateur, professional, prosperous and influential. An influential coach is a seasoned one who becomes 'a sought-after thought leader with dream clients calling them'. At this level, he promises you can take extended vacations, create income while you sleep, build a vast audience and a community of raving fans. Where do I sign?

'People spend time with me. We talk. And miracles occur.'

Rich Litvin, *The Prosperous Coach*

There are others in the coaching business who skip the training stage altogether. In my experience, they seem to charge the most, unencumbered by any awareness of what they don't know. The Dunning–Kruger effect again: the people who know the least are the most confident in their abilities.

Then there are also people who bandy the term around glibly, saying: '*I coached them on how to use the database.*' You didn't. You *showed* them how to use the database. It's called *training*. As I've explained in this book, you can't coach what someone doesn't know, and you can't coach someone out of a burning building, either. There's a time and a place for coaching and neither of these examples fits the bill.

Wherever we are at in our coaching '*journey*' – and that's the only time I've used that word in this entire book – we all have different ways of helping people. Clients rarely ask what method you use and how prestigious your training course was. They just want faith that you have their welfare at heart, trust that you are good at what you do and that you have their back – totally. Sometimes, the more you charge, the better they assume you are, the lure of the reassuringly expensive which works in other industries too.

I'm not here to promote or disparage the coaching profession, but I want to sound a warning bell about the responsibility that comes with it, especially the blurred boundaries between advice, therapy and coaching.

Management guru Warren Bennis has said: 'A lot of executive coaching is really an acceptable form of psychotherapy. It's still tough to say: "I'm going to see my therapist." It's okay to say: "I'm getting counselling from my coach".'

To be clear, coaching is neither counselling nor therapy. Anyone giving it a whirl, as either coach or coachee – the person being coached – must be careful to avoid confusing the two with coaching. We must avoid the temptation to be an armchair therapist if we don't have the right credentials, poking around where we have no business.

Just because we have overcome a challenge ourselves doesn't mean we have the skills to help others do the same. I've seen people attempt this and the stress of supporting someone else's struggles has set back their own recovery.

Sometimes only psychotherapy can help. That client shouldn't be coached at all.

What's the difference between coaching and therapy?

Coaches focus on the present and the future. We most often dwell on changing behaviour. We deal with problems where they pop up now and don't try to change the past. Therapists focus more on the past and the present and talk more about conscious thoughts or beliefs. Why do we behave the way we do? What's the mindset behind it?

Some of us are trained to operate in both realms to a lesser or greater degree. How we work with each coachee is driven by what we agree with them at the start of the contract and probably double-checked at the start of most individual sessions.

How do you want us to work together today?

What do you want to achieve by the end of the session?

What do you want to know at the end of the session that is unclear now?

Coaching is usually goal orientated. It's not simply a friendly chat. We are there to achieve something tangible and measurable. It is centred on the reasonable assumption that we can't change the past; we can change our reaction to it, and our beliefs about it. We can control how past experiences colour our life today and create obstacles to achieving those goals.

We may look back and speculate on where a problem stemmed from, but only if it is helpful to do so and is led by the client. I'd never push anyone to explore their backstory if they didn't want to. Once the client has clocked where a problem has started, we deal with how this experience led to a core belief about themselves that is causing them a problem today. This is what matters. We pick apart this core belief and challenge it with some data.

These are some examples of core beliefs.

I must be good.

I must please everyone.

I am not lovable/likeable.
People like me can't do this.
I can't trust anyone.
I am not good enough . . . and so on.

These are serious and deep-rooted beliefs we are dealing with. We need to handle these with the utmost sensitively. You don't need me to tell you how fragile people's mental health is.

Agreeing outcomes and how you will work together is called contracting. Frequently there are three people involved here: coach, coachee and the ultimate client, the person paying the bills and who judges whether they are getting a return on their hefty investment in time and money. How often and how much detail you communicate with the sponsor is another boundary to define. Whose side are you on?

During coaching training, a phenomenally long time goes on contracting. And as soon as a coaching relationship goes awry, you realise why. Nine out of ten times it's because people didn't contract properly. Expectations aren't aligned. The coachee hopes you'll tell them what to do, and they may confuse coaching and mentoring. Sometimes the organisational sponsor thinks you'll pass on sensitive information they can use for succession planning.

Sometimes, coaches can be manipulated for nefarious purposes. When I started my practice, I was almost misdirected on a coaching assignment with the vague goal of helping the person to 'figure out their career options'. The business wanted the person to decide to leave. The canny HR director thought coaching would smooth the path to a cheaper, easier exit. They wanted me to do the dirty work for them.

Unconscious processes in the coaching relationship

Coaching isn't just asking questions and hitting goals. Coaches have a responsibility to learn how the mind works and where we can do damage to the client, such as with emotional contagion – unwittingly spreading our own feelings – falling prey to confirmation bias and over-interpretation. This should be tackled via a robust, accredited training programme. Most importantly, we need to understand psychological processes, specifically transference relationships. These are the unconscious processes that go on between a coach and their client, just the same as happens between a therapist and their client.

Transference is when a person redirects their feelings about one person, usually a parental figure, onto someone else, such as the therapist/coach. This shows up most frequently in coaching when a client is keen to please me by doing their follow-up actions.

Countertransference is the opposite: the coach or therapist's emotional reaction to the client: our own stuff seeps through our boundaries. On a basic level, this means don't sleep with your client or fall in love with them. That's therapeutic rule number one.

But it also means not projecting our unmet needs onto the client. Many people in coaching or therapeutic roles come from family situations where other's needs took precedence over ours. We might even have been caretakers for parents or siblings at too young an age. Problems arise when we continue this caring and helping pattern into our work. Are we in the business of helping people because we are giving to others what we really want ourselves? Rescuing everyone else won't fix our stuff. None of us is our client's parent, and they aren't ours. These subconscious feelings make it important that we have proper supervision and support ourselves.

Don't impose your beliefs about yourself onto clients. For example, don't say they should spend more time with their family, that the role to which they aspire is out of their reach or that they should aim higher.

The coach might like or dislike their client because they remind them of someone else. A coach might feel the need to disclose unnecessary personal information to them, making it all about them, aiming for the client to meet *their* needs, instead of the opposite.

They might be too 'soft' with clients, which comes across as giving up on them. They may become too harsh, even bullying a client as 'tough love'. You may chivvy along the client: '*Is it really that bad?*' making them feel even more gaslighted because you aren't listening.

All of this compounds a client's problem and their core, unhelpful thinking about themselves.

It's almost impossible to discuss anything without tripping into 'mindset', psychological territory.

We can make things worse

Here's an example of how easy it is to cause emotional disturbance. You are a style coach, advising people on what to wear. Surely this is straightforward and practical with comments like: 'lemon yellow doesn't suit you'?

You can easily run into trouble despite your well-meaning intentions.

You need to earn a living, looking for clients to commit to work with you on a programme fee or monthly retainer. You need to get your client fully onboard with your services, so you light the spark by pointing out their problems, the consequences of them not changing.

Zena! Why do you wear baggy clothes that hide your shape?

Why aren't you more confident in your body?

When did you last feel good about yourself?

Why do you do this to yourself?

You can see how easy it is to drag up uncomfortable emotions or painful memories of early-life criticism and a failure to please. Everyone has off days, and we don't know what's going on in the rest of people's lives. Can you cope if they become distressed? And who'll take care of you?

Beware gurus, charlatans and hocus-pocus

We don't want a servant/supplier relationship with our clients; the power should stay equal. A red flag for me is if the client says a bit too often that 'I couldn't have done it without you'. I am a catalyst and it shouldn't be about me. It's a problem if it tips too much away from balance. A bit of gratitude is lovely, but we should be building self-efficacy, not encouraging dependency. That's a tricky line to navigate when you rely on repeat business to pay your bills.

There are thousands of wannabe self-help gurus out there, selling easy fixes to complicated and nuanced problems.

Positive psychology teaches us how to acknowledge all our emotions and stay resilient. It has been taken out of context by smiley-faced, Insta-meme loving practitioners. They claim they can make us happy all the time and that 'negative' emotions like sadness can, and must, be stamped out.

Grieving? Sorry for yourself? Depressed?

Cheer up! Choose happiness! Look at the bright side!

Say your affirmations! Fill your mind with positive thoughts!

This book is about managing your mindset, your interpretation of circumstances, but it's simply not possible to always be happy, nor is that even desirable. We can't expect to smooth out life's natural difficulties. Coaching interventions should help us ride the storm and not perceive a situation as worse than it is. It is natural to feel sad or upset or anxious at times. Believing those feelings to be bad, or that everyone else is constantly happy, makes us feel worse.

I once joined a virtual group coaching session, discussing obstacles to our business objectives. This was the first time we'd met. One person, getting visibly upset when describing their fear of failure, was asked: 'Where does that feeling come from?' They were encouraged to discuss their early childhood experiences in public during a few minutes on Zoom, by someone unqualified to deal with them. How did that person cope with the emotions stirred up? Who would help them afterwards? Who might they direct their anger or distress towards? This is unhelpful, at best, and potentially disastrous, at worst.

Misguided coaching ignores – and may even stir up – deep-rooted psychological problems. Every coach should be super aware of what they are dealing with and be qualified to handle it.

The urgency and dynamism of business today has made the dynamics of the coaching relationship even murkier. Coaches are expected to be more opinionated and directive, more of a mentor, bringing in our own experience more frequently. This suits me fine, but again it's all down to the contracting to define expectations and close supervision that ensures we keep our egos in check. It's never about us.

I'm increasingly being asked to accompany clients on meetings as part of their coaching programme. My major interest is efficiency, and observing how meetings are run is an inevitable part of seeing how time disappears. I'm also observing my client's influencing skills first-hand.

I usually give myself a talking-to, making sure I stay in my lane. I'm not there as their advocate or to meddle in decisions. What am I there for? Does everyone know that? Will they think it's weird if I say nothing? Are they expecting me to offer feedback on other people's performance? Or give my opinion?

Some coaches like to be in a more advisory role, similar to a civil servant pulling an MP's strings behind the scenes. They do a lot more of the talking.

'Get rid of this fucking guy: he doesn't know what the fuck he's doing,' Bill Campbell, leadership coach to Silicon Valley executives, is quoted as saying in the book *Trillion Dollar Coach* written about him by his admiring clients. We'd all love to say that sometimes. If that's your agreed contract, then go ahead. Just make sure you know what you are talking about.

The highly respected coach and lovely person Marshall Goldsmith is considered as the godfather of the coaching industry. He knows his role and keeps his ego in check: 'I don't come up with vaccines, but I coached the guy who came up with vaccines. I didn't turn around the Ford Motor Company, but I coached the guy that did.'

A land grab is underway at the top of the industry, with coaches fighting over big retainers from top-ranking leaders. Many of these coaches have doctorates in psychotherapy and had successful business careers before becoming coaches. They still have supervision from another senior coach. They are obsessed with their own professional development and never stop learning about the human mind.

But like other unregulated industries, there are charlatans at this level too, poisoning the well for others. Remember that follower numbers are no guarantee of credentials. Lured by the lucrative earnings of the coaching industry, some have motives that are more about their own profile than that of their client.

Problems arise when coaches ignore those vital therapeutic boundaries. When they want to be the hero of the narrative, to wield the power. Playing with people's minds is dangerous.

Charlatans take their clients 'to places they'd never go on their own'. Maybe a coachee didn't want to go to that place, but when a company is paying huge retainers, they want a return on their investment. Helping a coachee to achieve peace of mind is unlikely to cut the mustard. Lining up everyone's expectations can be a nightmare, so can picking up the pieces when coaching isn't done with care.

Where do you go from here?

What am I trying to tell you here? You can help people to change bad behaviour by asking more and speaking less. The golden rule is to avoid assuming that you know best. When in doubt, ask.

If, after reading this book, you are inspired to go all-in and qualify as a coach, then I can say you won't regret it. It will transform your relationships. But make sure you learn about psychological processes and evidence-based practice.

All training organisations should be certified by recognised bodies like the European Mentoring and Coaching Council, the International Coaching Federation, or the Association for Coaching.

Thank you for reading my book. Please email me on zena@zenaeverett.com if you want to talk through the pros and cons of becoming a professional coach, book me to speak about managing bad behaviour, or if you have comments on bad behaviour you have experienced. I'd love to hear from you.

I have one final magic question for you:

'*What have you learned about yourself after reading this book and what will you do differently as a result?*'

Resources

Burkeman, O. (2012) *The Antidote: Happiness for People Who Can't Stand Positive Thinking*, Canongate Books Ltd.

Ehrenreich, B. (2009) *Bright-Sided: How Positive Thinking Is Undermining America*, Picador USA.

International Coaching Federation (online) https://coachingfederation.org/blog/robust-growth-2023-global-coaching-study-results-are-in (accessed 15 July 2024).

Kirsh, N. (February 2022) *The Daily Beast*, on Marshall Goldsmith, see https://www.thedailybeast.com/inside-the-weird-high-powered-world-of-executive-coaches (accessed 15 July 2024).

Litvin, R. and Chandler, S. (2013) *The Prosperous Coach*, Maurice Bassett.

Rogers, J. (2024, 5th edition) *Coaching Skills: The definitive guide to being a coach*, Open University Press.

Schmidt, E., Rosenberg, J. and Eagle, A. (2019) *Trillion Dollar Coach, the Leadership Handbook of Silicon Valley's Bill Campbell*, John Murray.

Scoular, A. (2011) *The Financial Times Guide to Business Coaching*, FT Prentice Hall.

Index